FAMILIES
WRITING

ABOUT THE AUTHOR

Peter Stillman has written nine books (including the successful high school English text, *Writing Your Way*, and *Gilead*, his book of poems and journal entries), along with articles and poems too numerous to count. An editor and teacher as well as a writer, he travels the country speaking at writing conferences and seminars. He lives in upstate New York.

FAMILIES WRITING

PETER R. STILLMAN

Cincinnati, Ohio

"Marie's Unicorn" first appeared in the *Journal for the Education of the Gifted*, Vol. II, No. 2. Reprinted by permission.

"First-Day-of-School Quiet," by Susan Casper, which first appeared in *The Wisconsin Academy Review*, June, 1983, Vo. 29, No. 3, copyright © 1983 by *The Wisconsin Academy Review*, is reprinted by permission of *The Wisconsin Academy Review*.

"My Mother Pieced Quilts," by Teresa Palomo Acosta, copyright © 1975 by Teresa Polomo Acosta, first appeared in *Festival de Flor y Canto: an Anthology of Chicano Literature*, published by the University of Southern California Press, 1976. Reprinted by persmission.

Excerpts from "Dialogues" by Achille Chavée translated by Nicole Ball and reprinted from *Teachers & Writers* magazine. Copyright © 1988 by Teachers & Writers Collaborative. Reprinted by permission of Teachers & Writers Collaborative.

Various selections from *Writing Your Way*, copyright © 1984, by Peter Stillman, used by permission of Heinemann Education Books, Inc.

Excerpt from "Books for Your Most Important Audience," by Karon Phillips, which appeared in the November 1986 *Writer's Digest* is reprinted with permission of Karon Phillips.

96 95 94 93 92   5 4 3 2 1

Library of Congress Cataloging-in Publication Data

Stillman, Peter.
    Families writing/Peter R. Stillman.
        p.   cm.
    Includes index.
    ISBN 0-89879-525-7
    1. Authorship. 2. Family. 3. Family in literature. I. Title.
PN 145.S74   1989   89-5790
808'.042 – dc20   CIP

for Laura,
my daughter

O, the comfort, the inexpressible comfort of feeling safe with a person, neither having to weigh thoughts nor measure words, but pouring them right out just as they are, chaff and grain alike; certain that a faithful hand will take and sift them, keep what is worth keeping and then with the breath of kindness, blow the rest away.

—George Eliot,
Middlemarch

CONTENTS

I wrote this book partly because I know writing to be a powerfully good thing to do over a lifetime. Not, as we may have been taught, "good" in the same sense that prayer or personal hygiene is meant to be, in and of itself—not "good" to mean proper, approvable. I mean "good" as in *good for you*, like bran flakes or running fifteen miles a week. Writing, like running, is a form of conditioning; it toughens us, makes us resilient. When writers fall down, they don't break.

But I wrote this book mainly because it occurred to me one day years back that, aside from a fifth-grade report card, I had nothing in writing to prove that I existed between the day I entered the world and approximately age sixteen. Although I've never been challenged about that stretch of time—no one has doubted to my face that I began life prior to my getting a driver's license—it is a discomfiting fix to be in nevertheless. Why, I wondered, had my parents saved nothing of my childhood, my early writing, my attempts at drawing, notes from or about me as a child? For the same reason, I supposed, that they had given me nearly nothing of themselves on paper.

My mother and father were both intelligent, articulate people; it isn't that they were ignorant of writing's values. Quite the opposite: in their *milieu*, it was generally perceived that for writing to be of importance it must concern itself with matters beyond the mundane, that to write one must be both educated and gifted and, for that matter, must have led a life inordinately rich in experiences to record on paper. To write, in other words, one had to be a *Writer*. Except as measures of prowess in school, a child's writing thus counted for little; and as for my parents preserving anything of themselves, their world, on paper, such a notion would have struck them as ridiculous. They were, after all, working people, and there was for them nothing glamorous or exotic about toil. I suppose this is a commonplace irony—to have nothing of a mother and father other than a file of legal papers and some wordless, black and white photographs.

It's odd, ironic, that we so treasure family heirlooms—fret about whom they should be passed down to, agonize about possible breakage or loss, attach to some useless, often downright ugly artifact a value beyond dollars—while we mostly ignore family treasures made of *words*. Old letters, diaries, journals, schoolpapers if they are saved at all, most often end up in trunks in an inaccessible corner of the attic. And like our parents before us, we treat what little writing of this sort that *we* do with casual contempt.

I won't go so far as to say that families who ignore or devalue the uses and worth of writing in the home constitute cases of flawed kinship. But I will argue that writing should lie at the heart of any family—that if we don't value ourselves on paper, if we don't write to, for, about, and with family members, it must be because we haven't bothered to think deeply about what holds families together. Certainly it should have to do with our cherishing the imperishable voices from our family's past and adding our own voices to theirs.

So this is a book about just that—*why* to become a family that writes, along with a considerable detailing of *how*'s. This isn't one of those quick-fix, self-improvement courses. Writing doesn't lend itself to that kind of treatment, and don't let anyone convince you otherwise. It won't "improve" anybody in measurable ways, and even if it did, I can't imagine a more dreadful reason to be writing. Nor do I detail herein any new reasons for writing. To my satisfaction there aren't any, so I've instead talked about and illustrated some of the very old, very decent reasons to write, among them *to make a mark, to leave a record, to tell a story.*

There is a very good chance that if you and other family members young or old read this book and put it down long enough to try what I suggest, you'll discover for yourselves that there's something very rich about writing—that it's pleasurable, deeply gratifying, a remarkable way to get to know oneself and others better. Indeed, I hope you decide early in your experience with this book that you'd just as soon leave the reading to someone else—someone who may need further convincing—so that you can spend the time writing instead.

This is not a textbook. There are no rules, no gimmicks, no drills, no grammar exercises, no practice, no lists of rights and wrongs, no model sentences to copy out and imitate. Aside from my family, my biggest commitment is to helping others discover the inestimable value of writing in life. And rules and drills, practice sentences, and grammar exercises have nothing at all to do with this. In fact, there would be no reason for such a book if it weren't that nearly everybody by age fourteen has had the writer pounded clear out of them by year after year of such deadly stuff in the name of writing instruction. The best way to approach this book would be to pretend to be six or seven, back when you loved to write—when there was nothing to it; when creating a story was less complicated than reading one.

Even if you do choose to put the book aside in favor of writing, you'll find the reading to be quite engaging, I think, or so I endeavored to make it. There are also dozens of writers in here besides me. You won't know any of them;

they're people who write for themselves and their families, not for publication. One of the contributors is five, another is six, two are seven, and one is eight. Still another is nearly eighty-one. Throughout the following chapters I offer about sixty-five activities for people from roughly three years of age up to at least ninety-five. Yet, this isn't a fun-things-to-do-with-writing approach to writing. (It can be used in this mere way, but please don't.) There are plenty of amusing things to do in here, but writing doesn't amount to "things" to do—a bit of this, a dash of that. It is nothing like painting with numbers or putting together a momentarily puzzling puzzle. My four kids grew up to be wonderfully literate people simply because there was no escaping such a fate: they were surrounded from birth by evidences that writing and reading were not occasional amusements but the central stuff of life. While you might put it in other words, this is almost certainly what you'd like to happen in your family too. So undergirding the amusements I've maintained a thematic pressure to engage you and family members in long-range and/or frequently recurring kinds of writing. The long- and short-term activities fall together happily enough; the frivolous what'll-we-do-tonight? writing pastimes and the more serious journal keeping or memoir writing are complementary aspects of the same act.

The first chapter is a rationale—a reason *why*. It attempts to define what writing *is* (no small accomplishment if I could've pulled it off) and how it should figure in any family's more thoughtful activities. Chapter II is as convincing an inducement as I've ever seen to journal writing. Thus, there's no honest way out of it other than to begin a journal of your own and to convince others to do likewise. Much the same is true of the third chapter, which deals with letters and includes a gathering of my own, mostly for amusement's sake, mine and, I hope, yours as well. The next chapter, "Words as Gifts," details a number of reasons and ways for giving your writing to others. Chapter V is about family stories and ranges from lighthearted to rather serious reasons for tapping this inexhaustible resource. Chapter VI, "Poetry," could have amounted to a book. Instead, I kept it simple, more word play than serious poetry. The seventh chapter deals mostly with writing's hardware, from word processors down to thumbtacks. "More Reasons to Write," the last chapter, should more aptly have been titled "More Writing Activities," inasmuch as that's what it amounts to. Not that you'll need them; you'll be creating your own by this point or ignoring "activities" *per se* and concentrating on the sorts of writing that most fire your imagination, satisfy your hunger to write.

(Afternote: It may strike some as odd that I've not included a chapter dealing with genealogy. Indeed, I had originally planned to do so, but initial research disclosed that [a] basic genealogy has relatively little to do with writing, except incidentally; but even if it did, [b] it would have been impossible to put together anything truly useful within the span of a chapter. Instead, I've included an appendix that lays out basic resources and initial steps for those interested in pursuing the subject.)

ACKNOWLEDGMENTS

There is an established format for acknowledging others' contributions to the making of a book: one is expected first to thank the most significant figure in the venture, the one "without whom this book couldn't possibly have been written"; and then, trailing that one by a nose, the person "whose help was invaluable"; following this, in show position, is the somebody whose "thoughtful reading" or "critical commentary" made all the difference. From here, one simply casts a net of thank-yous meant to scoop in everybody, including your folks for having you in the first place and down to the postman for delivering correspondence from people without whom this book couldn't possibly have been written. A person is a piker if he or she doesn't list at least fifteen or so contributors whose beneficent influences figured in the making of the text. Nevertheless, I've held it to three, to avoid clutter, not thanks.

Vital to this venture is Bingo Tartaglia, who happened to notice that I had fallen asleep under his Studebaker at the Fish & Game Club clambake back in 1957 and thus did not run over my head. And while I don't doubt for a minute that I could have written this book without the help of Ann Allen Stillman, my wife, it wouldn't have come out the same way. "I don't know what goes where," I told her, so she spread the whole manuscript on the living room floor like a messy hand of solitaire and began moving pieces around until she found the order that had eluded me. There cannot be gratitude enough for that kind of help. The only other person central in my thanks is Jean Fredette, whose consistent decency as editor and friend is what used to characterize book publishing long, long ago.

CHAPTER ONE

Why Write?

It's tempting to fill a page or two here with sermonizing, to deplore the falling-away of writing as a family activity, and to make persuasive connections between this and the erosion of family ties generally. Closer to the truth, though, is that only incidentally have individuals ever consciously used writing *per se* to maintain close-knit ties among family members. It takes perceptive word lovers to sense what a powerful family bonding agent writing can be, and if you're not one of them no amount of sermonizing will convert you. Therefore, I'll avoid any tub-thumping about family writing, on the assumption that we're joined here, if only for the few moments it takes to skim this prefatory rambling, by a mutual interest in the subject.

I don't know of a greater, wiser gift than words written down. Years back when my children were small, I somehow sensed the need to give them words of mine. In retrospect, it's clear that I was seeking ways to keep them and me together beyond the fleeting span of time between early childhood and their pushing off into the wider world, into lives mostly separate from mine. I expressed this need in a homely enough way: a series of sketches, each labeled "When I Was Your Age" and captioned with a sentence or two about what it was like to be seven or eight or twelve back when I was a kid.

I don't know how many were produced in all, but for years no birthday or Christmas passed without each child receiving a framed present containing a simple cartoon and a paragraph's worth of nostalgia. One, I remember, depicted a solitary kid trudging down a deserted street in winter. The caption said, in essence, *I had lonely moments too: everybody does.* Another was of an eight-year-old holding a b-b gun and looking in dismay at a dead cardinal. The text was about my first gun and the unforgivable act I'd committed with it. Still another was a sketch of a kid (me) being thrown from a horse. One of my sons had recently had a similar experience with *his* first horse, so it seemed an appropriate enough comment on a shared father-son mishap.

When I was your age, I smoked my first cigarette.
It was a Camel. I stole it from my mother, sat
on my favorite rock, and lit up. I loved every
minute of it.

I'd like to think that, come Christmas or a birthday, my children looked forward to their "When I Was Your Age" present more eagerly than any other gift. Probably not, though. To a typical nine-year-old, a two-dimensional memento should reasonably come in a distant second to a bicycle or a pair of skiis. I do know this, however: long after all the treasures of Christmases and birthdays past had been broken or outgrown, those little messages remained, and today they hang on walls far from here. Nor do I over-value my words when I venture that none of those kids would part with even the crudest "When I Was Your Age" for any sum, for how can you over-value written words that daily evoke a vital truth: I belong, I am loved, I am a central figure in that most enduring of human institutions, *family?* Furthermore, I'd guess that someday those sketches will amuse descendants of mine I won't be around to meet in person.

For anyone who takes it seriously, writing is a mystical business. Far more than a medium for conveying and storing information or even as a means for creative expression, writing keeps us *alive.* Yes, I mean it is a vital business, a way to keep us close and thriving as a family. But I also mean that writing propels us past the clutch of years we'll spend here on this planet and into a

When I was your age, my grandmother still had an icebox instead of a refrigerator. Ice kept the food cold then, big blocks of it delivered by the iceman from a horse-drawn wagon. There is no ice left in the world as cold as his.

vastly larger dimension of time. Write to and with your loved ones to establish the importance of your family *now,* and you are unavoidably writing to and with members of your family *hence.* Any family is organically anxious to perpetuate itself, and one of the best ways to do so is through writing.

BOTHERING TO WRITE

Even if I would, I couldn't shake ancestral words from mind for what they bring to me of their authors. On my desk is a small, privately printed volume, *Miscellaneous Compositions,* written by William Stillman. It was published in 1852 and was intended mostly for his family. William was a self-taught clockmaker, a good one. In fact, he tells me that he made his first clock when he was only eighteen and had never laid eyes on a timepiece; and furthermore, that the project so obsessed him, "It made me very poor in flesh." It isn't hard to conjure him in my mind's eye, this fellow New Englander and relative, tinkering the nights away in a dark corner of his father's blacksmith shop. You can't help but admire such singlemindedness, any more than you can avoid a rush of sympathy when a year later his young wife died and he wrote (to me, my children, theirs) "No earthly thing could ever be/Compared with her sweet company." Or a chuckle when William observes about another relative of ours, Uncle Joseph Stillman, "I never heard him preach but once, and I never wanted to hear him again."

I'm glad to have made his acquaintance, and proud too. Seems to me the world would be a better place if we had a few more of William's kind about: loving, witty, diligent, and wise enough to sense that his writing it down might someday matter to me.

Most of us lack that wisdom. Most of us, at least, lump writing for, to, with, and about our families with other high-minded things we intend to do, such as cleaning the attic or giving up martinis. Or, just as bad, we wait for something to happen, something worth the bother, when the liberating truth about this kind of writing is that the mundane matters of life are what matter. I'd rather know William for his tinkering and his toothaches than for some uncharacteristic deed, however remarkable. We're mostly what we daily do and think about, and thus there's always much to record, far more than anyone could ever put to paper.

Two people come to mind as I write this. One is an auto mechanic named Bill Anteman. He somehow found out that I was an English teacher, so whenever I stopped by his shop, he'd pull from his wallet a much-folded, grease-smudged sheet of paper and ask that I read and comment on it. Always they were poems, and, judged by literary standards, not very good ones. They dealt with various family-related matters — the birth of a child, a vacation trip, a marriage. "Good stuff," I'd tell him, amused to discover how he spent his evenings. What I was too obtuse to realize back then was that I was in the presence of a *real writer*, a man who, without education or some quirky knack for writing, had learned the value of capturing the stuff of his life on paper. What I also didn't sense was that Bill was in the process of creating a vastly heightened sense of family literacy at his kitchen table every night. Especially when we write for and about the audience closest to us in their very presence, something of the act rubs off: it becomes familiar, comfortably right. (He eventually published a collection of his verse, which he titled *Notes from a Greasy Pen.* Last I heard, he'd sold out two printings.)

The other person who comes to mind is Mildred Dales, whose little self-published book, *Letters from Grandma,* amounts to just that, a series of letters to her grandchildren, Jeff and Holly. They're neither sloppily sentimental nor self-consciously literary. Mrs. Dales writes simply about simple matters, and manages in the process to create a priceless family treasure. She writes about such trivia as what bathroom facilities used to be like. ("One day Aunt Minnie was coming to visit and we were trying to have everything in order.

My brother Harvey was sent upstairs to gather the slops. As he started down the stairs someone yelled, 'Here she comes.' Harvey stumbled on the top step and poured the contents down the full flight, never missing a step!") About how her father played pranks on his wife. ("If she were sitting down peeling apples and he came in she would probably find herself tied to the chair with her apron stings.") About ice boxes, hair care, housecleaning, cellars, automobiles, even coping with menstruation sixty years ago; and angrily, powerfully about growing old. She didn't wait for the big stuff; she captured the homely aspects of life instead and offered it to people she cared about. You should be doing the same thing.

WRITING TO LEARN

Always as a teacher it perplexed me when students responded to my encouragements with, "But there's nothing to write about." For most of them it wasn't laziness, however; they'd been schooled over years to understand writing as a remote and unfigurable artform no more attainable for them than walking on water. There was real writing, the stuff that writers did, and there was schoolwriting. The latter amounted to sticking apostrophes and commas in the right places in drill sentences (Is it "Harold the bill collector is here," or "Harold, the bill collector is here"?) and to knocking out vacuous book reports and five-paragraph themes to keep from flunking. So when they observed that there's nothing to write about, it was an honest enough response, for that's what most kids then and now are schooled to write about—long strings of nothings.

People who learn the real uses of writing early in life and are sustained in them at home have relatively little trouble with school writing. If young people enter school already rich in literate practices, they simply won't be taken in by baloney. This isn't even a faintly arguable assertion; I've seen too much proof. Expose children to the opposite—a home where nobody writes except grudgingly, perfunctorily—and you will have done much to convince them that indeed there's nothing to write about. And your family and the human family generally will be the poorer for it. Russian poet Yevgeny Yevtushenko wrote, "In any man who dies there dies with him his first snow and kiss and fight." Not if he gets it on paper, though; not if he's encouraged from early childhood to write it down.

I don't intend that this book be used to help youngsters earn flashy scores on standardized tests, because (a) as a society we're already far too unhealthily obsessed with scores; and (b) I've never seen a standardized writing test that had anything to do with writing's real purposes. Besides, nearly any kid raised in a home where everybody writes is bound to score well on such tests no matter how ridiculous they are.

The truth is that writing is a central means of learning, whether it's academic or personally revelatory. It's as much for finding out as for reporting. Writing is for fun, too; it was never meant to be the ponderously serious medium that educators have made of it. Thus, there's some rather goofy stuff in here, for both youngsters and adults. Won't do anybody a bit of harm, nor will the many other family-oriented writing activities I've included. You'll find some more engrossing than others, but none is dull, off-puttingly elaborate, condescending, or idiotic. And every one of them is meant to pull families closer together and help to maintain them that way. Whatever else writing may be for, it is emphatically for that.

You don't have to "know how to write" to write. Beyond mastering the rudiments of literacy, which most of us did by fourth grade, there isn't any reliable list of skills to be learned; we become writers whenever we put pen to paper and attempt to say honestly and artlessly whatever comes to mind. It doesn't have much to do with intelligence or innate talent either. It has to do with rediscovering what you knew beyond doubt at age five or six: that you could write as well as anybody and that doing it was mostly a joy. Most people are convinced they don't know how to write, when all they really mean is that they didn't do too well in English class. The truth is, there's absolutely no connection between one and the other. You don't have to know a noun from a verb or how to spell *preposterous* to write richly to and with your family or anybody else. For now, take that on faith; I'll prove it sooner or later.

WRITING ACROSS SPACE AND TIME

Separation for whatever reason — business trips, hospital stays, even and especially legal separation/divorce — is made more bearable through writing. I'm freshly astonished and saddened whenever I find still another divorced parent who relies only on regulated visits and greeting cards to maintain ties with his or her children, instead of bridging the distance with writing. One divorced parent I know maintained a zany correspondence with his kids that took the form of a two-way advice column. At frequent intervals he'd cook up a light-hearted list of tips for each youngster. They'd respond in kind. Here are samples of his observations:

- The Tooth Fairy pays more for molars.
- Always haul water up from a well. Don't go down after it.
- If it doesn't break with a light tap, it's probably not an egg.
- Try not to spit when you yell.
- Stay out of alphabetical orders.
- People who keep saying, "Ha-ha, that's all *you* know" don't have alot of friends.
- There are alot of jerks running around saying "alot" is twowords.

Silly stuff, to be sure. But it, along with other kinds of inventive writing notions, kept words and affections flowing. I can't prove it, but I'd like to think that this father's writing to the children from whom he was separated by many miles and often months—and their writing back—was the central reason why he and they never experienced the gradual letting go so deplorably common to broken homes.

Most parents remember a child's first word. Indeed, it's one of the requisite specifics we're expected to log in the blue- or pink-covered "Baby Book" provided by diaper services or grandmothers. Other data include weight at birth, first tooth, first step, guests at the first birthday party, etc. Such books are filled with labeled spaces, in which mother or dad dutifully jots information until soon enough we put off doing it and store the thing in the attic, half of the blanks unfilled.

This is entirely reasonable. Kids were never meant to be reduced to data and stored in pre-captioned spaces. It goes against nature. It also goes against the writer in us, which secretly resents being told what to write when and where. The best that can be said about baby books is that they're better than nothing.

WRITING TO REMEMBER

A few years back during a drive in late autumn my wife's 4-year-old grandson started chuckling to himself in the back seat.

"What are you laughing at?" I asked him.

"November," he told me.

"What's so funny about that?" I said.

"I just changed it to Yesvember," he said.

"Write that down," I said to my wife sitting next to me. (She's so used to that request that she carries a little scratch pad in her bag when we go off on a ride.) Because, although I've heard funnier lines from little kids, Ryan's observation was one more poignant proof that as we age, our vision narrows. *Yesvember.* It did seem to brighten up the day. In a few years I'll give the word back to him, maybe in the form of the poem it inspired:

Yesvember

Yes *comes*
from places
in the sky
and settles. Two
brown leaves
rasp it. Geese
whistle yes
down a pale wind.

Snow is letters.
I let
the y's and e's and esses
sting my eyes,
and taste their
cold agreements
on my tongue.

Ryan will also eventually discover that he figures importantly in my journal, which is for stretches a log of his zany observations about such disparate matters as corporal punishment ("Spankin' don't do me no good"), getting dressed ("Hear that song in my zipper?"), the nature of celestial bodies ("Stars don't have no hair"), astrophysics ("Clouds are for holdin' rainbows down"), and relativity ("Later is a long time from now").

What family member's funny or touching never-to-be-repeated observation have you jotted down today, this week? Why not? Here's one vital truth no one in the writing business would dream of disputing: *You won't remember it if you don't write it down.* And a corollary of that truth is that you'll be sorry as blazes if you don't.

RUNNING FROM WRITING

Here, for convenience's sake, is a list of reasons for not writing.

- I don't have the time.
- I never was any good at it.
- My desk is a mess.
- My typewriter needs a new ribbon.
- My typewriter is broken.
- I can't think of anything to write about.
- I'm too tired right now; I'll do it tomorrow.
- I have to be inspired to write.
- Maybe when we can afford a word processor...

What these excuses have in common is that they're all baloney. Substitute a word here and there and it becomes a list of reasons for not putting out the garbage or making love. Uncle William didn't have a typewriter and he didn't major in English. As for inspiration, most of it is lodged in the business end of a pencil; like a stick-shift car with a weak battery, all it takes is a little push to get it going.

Despite all the hype, electronic word processors don't teach a person anything much about writing, especially how to get better at it. They're hotrod typewriters, and if I'm oversimplifying here, it isn't by much. I'll get into what they *are* good for a littler farther along. For now, keep in mind that this book's primary purpose is to get you and your family engaged in writing—to steer you toward arriving at your own conclusions about its long- and short-term values. It isn't to sharpen your writing skills, to improve your punctuation, to enhance your income, or to get you published. Any or all of these things could very well come out of your taking this book seriously, but approximately the same results would eventually occur if you simply wrote *more.* The only reliable way to write *better* is to keep at it. Machinery has nothing to do with it.

As for having nothing to write about, it is one of the two most frequently proffered excuses for not putting words to paper (the other being, "I always hated English"). But it is never the case, not for a five-year-old child and certainly not for you. Like it or not, you are a camera that never runs out of film. You'll eventually discover that there is far too much to put on paper— that even if you kept at it diligently for twelve hours a day, seven days a week, you'd come away frustrated about how much more there is to write about.

WRITING TO FIND OUT

Two years ago I used writing to arrive at a decision about which brand of pickup truck to buy. No, it wasn't that I jotted down numbers to compare prices or wrote manufacturers for more information. The first thing I did was divide a sheet of paper into two columns, one headed "Why," the other, "Why not." At this point I wasn't even sure I needed a new truck, and this seemed a simple way to round up the swarm of contrary concerns buzzing in my head and get them out on paper where they could be sorted and evaluated. I make it sound more methodical than it was, however; what came out of the experience wasn't a clear-cut answer but the equally important discovery that I worry too much—that Hamlet-like I tend to agonize rather than act. The proof was indisputable: five pages of *why's* and *why not's* that I'd quite unconsciously balanced one against the other to avoid reaching a decision. It was useful to know, rather than merely suspect about myself.

A couple of years before I'd used the same technique to help choose one brand of computer over another. Precisely the same thing happened; I concluded the exercise tied in even worse knots. Finally I gave my wife, who is computer-illiterate, a brochure on each machine and said, "Which one do you think is better-looking?" She said the beige one was, so I bought it. Took her all of 3 or 4 seconds to make up my mind. Left to my listing I'd still be at it.

The point is that writing fosters vision (although it's usually, erroneously, put the other way around). It is the most powerful means of discovery accessible to all of us throughout life, which makes it doubly ironic that it is taught and used in schools almost exclusively as a means for printing out what we're already charged with knowing. British novelist E. M. Forster's rhetorical question, quoting an anonymous elderly woman, about writing to discover is familiar to nearly everyone in the writing business: "How can I know what I think till I see what I say?"

I've learned over years to write whenever I'm baffled or angry or depressed. It isn't so much for the therapeutic benefit of distraction (although that too); it's mainly that *something* is going to rise to the surface, something forgotten or unrealized, an unforged connection, a new way to look at a plague-y matter, a lovely, powerful line, a deepened sense of self or another. If this sounds fanciful, a trendy formula for performing right- and left-brain tricks or solving life's problems in ten easy steps, let me assure you that it isn't. Writing is a way of thinking, a passage into the mind, where the riddle lies. It is often far better than talk or solitary musing, for these two mediums lack palpable shapes, and furthermore, mind and pen sometimes seem to move in the same reflective rhythms. We pause on the page, confronting its vacancy, much as the mind seems to pause, unsure of the way; and then the words come, often disordered hordes of them, drawing us from our narrowly rational intent, skewing the plan. So it is with the mind.

Writing, in other words, takes us where we might not otherwise venture. I remember beginning the following owed and aimless letter to a close friend with a paragraph about...about nothing really, an aimless, lighthearted paragraph meant to fill up space and amuse. There remains for me no reasonable way to explain how that letter swung away from prattle and became a poignant revelation about my late father, making clear to me for the first time an aspect of the man I'd never before understood. Much of writing, like much of thought itself, is irrational, a way through the looking glass, where such matters often dwell.

I don't offer this letter as an example of good writing. It was written hurriedly and without any conscious intent beyond fulfilling an obligation and keeping in touch. I didn't know until after it was done what it said. This may be hard to swallow, for most of us have been schooled to worship the topic sentence, to stick first to last to the dictates of a preconceived outline—to believe that we must *know* before we write the first word what the last one will be, along with all that will be contained between. It is terribly hard to shake these convictions, for they have a compelling logic to them: writing is an entirely rational system, and systems require plans, steps, an order. If you cannot readily perceive and follow such a system, you are a defective writer.

What this fails to allow for is that excepting the more mechanical forms of writing—standardized reports, routine job-related writing such as business letters—*writing is thinking.* Much of the time, therefore, we simply cannot know in advance what the writing will say, any more than we can know where our thoughts will take us. If you are curious to find out what writing can do for you, write and find out. Put any stultifying, paralyzing textbook notions out of mind. Watch what happened when I did:

Dear Frank,

God gave me little to go on and that is a sorry fact. I do not have the equipment to excel in anything. Sometimes I even wake up perfectly willing to be dead and remembered, like Fred Allen or Enrico Fermi, who had gifts, God-given gifts. Nobody is going to remember me. My own children will forget. Where is our father buried? one of them will call up and ask another. What father? he will say. Because you do not remember people whose only gift is a natural part on the right, even if they are your father. I will be admitted to Heaven with a shrug. Never mind that I am wearing a maybe 300-dollar suit, I am nothing but a 40 regular, the sixth one today. Some mornings I wake up feeling like a piece of junk mail with Ed McMahon's picture on it.

My father had a smallness of vision too. He never let himself dream large, give voice to any wish that wouldn't fit within the modesty of the moment. Yet he was not merely what he seemed—a humble, hardworking man. I would find it easier to cherish him for those simple-to-admire qualities, to hang him in the mind's gallery as the embodiment of the parental myth. Here is father home, come out of the night beyond the parlor window, the farthest streetlight, and he will gather us in with hands that bear fine little maps of grime and toil's scars. He will smell faintly of gasoline and burning oil, and I will think of it as the smell of work.

He grew up in an unimaginably large and confusing world. In fact I do not think people in his station thought it a world in the same sense we do. It was mostly a bewildering abstraction: there was an Africa, but no there wasn't; it was in a book, but so were names of stars one couldn't see. He left school in ninth grade, somewhere near the middle of the Great War. He'd been on the basketball team. I used to tell friends that my father was a star basketball player. I didn't know what else to boast about him. You couldn't say, My father works very hard—it would only be shouted down by others saying the same thing about their fathers—although it might have pleased him to know that I'd thought to say it, that I attached a pride to it.

I often wonder what he would have been like as a soldier. When I was small I sometimes wished he were in the war. I had hazy, stirring notions about war, about his being a hero. Once, my mother told me, he charged out from a crowd of onlookers and threw himself on a man who had disarmed a policeman and was beating him with the latter's nightstick. Then he ran away, she said. He didn't want anyone to find out who he was.

He liked books. He read to me, took me often to the library. It wasn't that he read that much himself; I don't remember ever seeing him with a novel. It was that he believed there was something in books that made you better than you would otherwise be. That strikes me now as being terribly sad, because he seemed to have been saying, Here, it's too late for me to be any more than what I am, and therefore these can be of no use to me; they're meant to make you different, better.

It was one of many ways he pushed me from him. He was a master mechanic and yet would never let me help him, never answer my eager questions about how engines worked. I could not use a tool in his presence without being derided for my ineptitude. He came from a time when you were either a mechanic or a professional person, when you either worked with your hands or your brain. There was no reason for one to acquire the skills or knowledge of the other. And because of this narrow, necessary vision, he could only push me from his world without helping me to perceive its alternatives. He meant me to discover them in places he felt unworthy and unknowledgeable of.

I think my father could have been nearly anything — poet, painter, physician — if he had not been so thoroughly absorbed by the age he lived in that it became impossible — as literally impossible as if he had been sightless. This is why I find it hard to remember him simply and with easy affection, the way one is supposed to remember his father. If at least he had read beyond his own boyhood, we could have talked about books, used them as a bridge across the gulf he imagined between him and me. I would have loved to remember such conversations, loved remembering his going upstairs to bed with a book in his hand.

I do remember his taking me to the kind of places he felt housed a power to educate and transform. You can take a child to museums and galleries and historical monuments because they are in themselves interesting places to visit on a Sunday, or because you believe them to be oracular, to contain a magic to which children are wonderfully susceptible. Looking back, I read into those Sundays his quiet urgency that I absorb before it was too late — before I hardened into another him.

He was all terribly, hopelessly wrong to perceive himself so meagerly, just as he was wrong to think he could propel a son so firmly from him into what he imagined to be an infinitely more beautiful world than his own that he would ever become for me a fondly simple clutch of memories.

I don't know how all this started, except that it was still too early to mow the lawn. . . .

When you don't *know* what to write about, you're forced to write with *faith* — faith in the process, faith that something will come, occasionally something you'll be vastly richer for. It might be argued that in the instance above, I must have known about these aspects of my father and how they colored our relationship long before I wrote an early morning letter about them. Indeed, I must have known something of them. Had I not, the letter would have been pure invention, a fiction. This letter, though, is a surprisingly powerful *revision* of those aspects. I had never seen them or him in this light before. It took perhaps an hour to write this letter. Would you trade an hour of your life for the discovery that your father's seeming rebuffs were an expression of his love?

WRITING PROMPTS

Try this. Now, not when you've finished reading or walked the dog or cleaned the oven. Take an empty sheet of paper and draw a floorplan of the first house or apartment you remember living in. It needn't be to scale; the roughest approximation will do. Label each room, either in terms of its function, e.g., "kitchen," or whose territory it chiefly was: "Tom's room," "Dad's shop," "Mom's sewing room." (If it was more than one floor, do a separate sketch for each.)

Next, use each room's label as the heading of a column. Without pondering and in reckless haste, scribble down a list of words and short phrases under each heading. Don't wait for the right word; there isn't any. Nor are there any wrong ones; if you list as many recollected feelings and sensations as furnishings, fine. And don't fill up one column before going to the next. Jump around. For once, follow the irksomely skittish, nonlinear way your mind works. More don't's:

- correct or erase anything
- stop and think about anything
- even consider whether or not anything's spelled or punctuated correctly
- worry about neatness
- call up a sibling or parent to ask whether you're right or wrong about where the second bathroom was
- figure this is too silly to bother with.

Now look. Are you surprised at any of your entries? Circle those that are even faintly intriguing. Don't concern yourself with what brought them to the surface. Instead, make a few connections; draw lines between those entries that seem even vaguely related, whether or not the relationship is based on recollected fact or something you can't quite put your finger on. Take any paired terms now and put them at the top of a fresh sheet of paper.

Start writing, again at helter-skelter speed. Not necessarily about the items that head the page, but about whatever images, feelings, recollections they bring to mind. Don't worry about accuracy, or even about telling what you believe to be the truth. In an important sense, it is nearly impossible to lie on paper, especially at high speed.

I'm going to do this exercise with you. Like you, I won't know what's going to come out. Whatever does, I won't change a word of it.

The gabled window above the built-in chest was high enough so that to look out I had to push aside the clutter of toys and stand atop the oak lid. It was synonymous somehow with the boredom I nearly always felt in that small room at the top of the stairs; for it looked out on the foot of an empty street, a street without children and thus without a sound or movement that attracted me. It was the same with the kitchen window over the sink, my drying the supper dishes, too short to see out to the yard, the road beyond, still most evenings as the street that fronted our small house. It may not be a terrible thing for a small child to live in a nearly childless neighborhood, but it is a powerful thing nevertheless. My only playmate was the girl next door, a dreadful little tease. Thus, I was without any real companion, and by the time I was old enough to venture into the world at the bottom of the hill I was wholly ignorant of the social structure of male society, of the games and rituals other boys were comfortable with. I could not, for example, dribble a basketball, nor did I have the courage to steal an apple from a fruitstand, nor could I even spit with accuracy, inhale a cigarette, swear with easy confidence, or sense when I was expected to stand and fight. I'm still, 40 years later, inept at these things; too soon it becomes too late.

Looking back at your list, perhaps you can now sense that pairing any term with any other one would have generated something meaningful. (My terms were *windowseat* and *dark beyond the kitchen,* neither of which found their way into the paragraph.) Listing is a remarkable generator for any writer. We use it all the time, but in such innocuous ways it doesn't occur to us that we're actually using our lists to *think.* Consider the shopping list. How is it that when we jot down "pumpernickel," another item leaps to mind—mayonnaise or marmalade, which in turn seems to compel other connections? It isn't that we carry the list written in mind; it's that the very act of listing is a process of thought, of association, even if we are not aware of it or would avoid it. If you let it, this simple technique will nearly always propel you past whatever forms of paralysis set in when you confront a blank sheet of paper, and it will almost always give the lie to that familiar old excuse, "There's simply nothing to write about today."

The chances are good that if you worked your way through this exercise, what came out on paper wasn't really about a dwelling place; it was instead about something more or other than that. It was almost unavoidably about *you,* even if "I" never once appeared in the writing. Although each of us believes him- or herself to be unique as a snowflake, too few understand writing to be the one readily available way for sharpening and distilling this vague sense of singularity—for accumulating the random bits of self, regularly, faithfully, that will provide not only momentary revelations but over time a deepened sense of who we really are behind the face we put on for the world. (Which is why we should not throw away writing. This is another school habit, a particularly tragic one.)

I begin to make this sound like heavy going and it's not. The kinds of writing addressed throughout this book have a variety of intents, but they have in common a recreational quality; they should be engaging, even fun. Do keep this in mind. Like other forms of recreation, writing may seem more like a chore at first; you may strain for effect, over-concentrate, backslide into schoolroom anxieties about being "right." Give it time; you'll start liking it, liking the myriad shapes and sounds of yourself on paper.

Why not agree to do some more jottings like the one you just completed and to suggest to other family members young and old that they try them too? A week's worth at least. Here are some suggestions, although they're meant only to be prompts or guides, suggestive of topics more directly appropriate to you:

- a list of every car you've owned, followed in each case by a short comment about the vehicle.
- a list of every dog, cat, gerbil, parakeet and/or orangutan that has figured in your life, with a phrase's worth about each.
- the names of fellow students in kindergarten or first grade. (Note that as you jot names, other names will come to you. Writing is a powerful memory jogger.) If this seems beyond you—it's not but it may seem so—then list a dozen teachers you've had, and let them evoke—on paper—whatever free-form associations come to mind.
- list the ten most important dates in your life—birthday not to count. Write about one or two of them.
- list ten things you know you should give or throw away but can't bear to part with. Explain (to yourself) your connections with at least half of them.
- write about five people you've always disliked and why. (Also allow for your feelings to change if that's the way the writing appears to be moving you.)
- list ten projects you've been putting off and how and when you'll accomplish at least two of them. (But if you end up writing about your being a procrastinator or how your family has devised ways over the generations of avoiding unpleasant chores, go with it.)
- jot down five decisions you've been putting off. Write your way into making one of them.
- list five or six people to whom you should write a letter. (This isn't necessarily the same as "owing" a letter.) Write to the first two people on the list,

or at least explain to yourself why you haven't written and what you'd probably say if you did.
- now write to the other three or four.
- write without pausing to think about four or five life-long frustrations. Then jot down what you've ever done about any two of them.
- and what you'll do about another one or two. And finally why you avoided dealing with the other(s).
- in briefest form, list as many situations as you can think of where you failed to say or do what you knew the occasion called for. Don't stop at ten; there are hundreds, e.g., when you were too shy to ask, when your date behaved boorishly, situations involving the boss who drew pleasure from bullying you, the condescending headwaiter, the rude cabby, the pious hypocrites, pollyannas, high-pressure salespeople, telephone solicitors, con artists, cat lovers, door-to-door gospel peddlers.
- now pick out five and tell them what you should have told them then. (Two-word responses not to count.)
- list five times you've lied, along with at least one fleshed-out proof that lying doesn't pay.

These lists are to be points of departure, just as the listing of rooms was. You should return to them too, whenever you feel that you've run dry of subject matter or faith in your writing. Both feelings are irrational, which in no way diminishes their occasional intensity. Read this book, more or less going along with me/it, and you won't need external prompts like these, except rarely.

• • • • • • • • • •

Even if you're a teacher by profession, please don't use this book in teacherly ways. Don't, that is, stress correctness over substance in others' writing, offer critiques, issue assignments, refer to anyone's writing as a "paper," ask a family member of any age to "pass in" his or her "work," write comments of any kind on a piece of writing without an express request from its author, ever, ever use red ink, circle words, insert question marks, employ such handy-hideous shorthand as "awk," "sp," "expl," or, for Heaven's sake, put a grade on another's writing—unless you wish to mortify, dishearten, and as well to pervert the promise implicit in this book.

If this stance seems recklessly permissive, consider that the National Council of Teachers of English urges much the same of parents. In the pamphlet *How to Help Your Child Become a Better Writer* are these pointers:

Be as helpful as you can in helping children write. Talk through their ideas with them; help them discover what they want to say. When they ask for help with spelling, punctuation, and usage, supply that help. Your most effective role is not as a critic but as a helper. Rejoice in effort, delight in ideas, and resist the temptation to be critical. . .

Praise the child's efforts at writing. Forget what happened to you in school and resist the tendency to focus on errors of spelling, punctuation, and other mechanical aspects of writing. Emphasize the child's successes. For every error the child makes, there are dozens of things he or she has done well.

(Note: This useful pamphlet is available free from: NCTE Order Dept., 1111 Kenyon Rd., Urbana IL 61801.)

● ● ● ● ● ● ● ● ● ●

CHAPTER TWO

Journals and Journaling

If writing had an essence, a pure form, it would for me be most observable in the act of making an entry in a journal. It is a private act, accomplished for and by the self and yet, ideally, unself-conscious. Nothing matters beyond the act itself—not neatness nor spelling nor other mechanical errors, and certainly not style or subject. It amounts to a congenial transaction between you and an empty page that nearly all journal keepers I know look forward to. And although I can't substantiate the claim, I'm certain that if we had learned as children to keep a journal, somehow our world by now would be a far saner place.

Years ago I began a journal because I moved one winter into a small cabin high on a wind-blasted mountain far from civilization and without running water or electricity. I cultivated a number of rituals and routines, mostly to keep from going crazy. Journal keeping was one of them, at its inception no more significant to me than splitting firewood. Soon enough, however, I realized I'd been a fool to wait for some silly extreme to present itself before I began a journal; and also that unlike the other routines I'd concocted, this one had become utterly compelling.

In fact I dug through the original cabin journal about three years back and found enough material to fashion a small book about life on a mountaintop. Even if I hadn't, though, the thing would be invaluable to me for a host of reasons:

- To write decently (not professionally, simply somewhere near saying what you mean to) requires a near-daily involvement with writing. This is not ventured speculatively; it's a rock-hard fact. And there are few places to do this on a daily basis other than in a journal.
- Generally, we don't possess nearly the power to recall or retain details of an experience that we think we do. To remember—to evoke the particu-

lars of the past at will. If I were to be granted one wish, this would be the one I'd request. How many moments have you and I lived through that at the time affected us so powerfully we knew we'd never forget them? And of them, how many are all but gone, softened to an indistinct haze? Among other things, writing is a substitute for our fallible memories; committing experiences to paper while they are still fresh is the only reasonable way I know to retain them relatively free from time's erosions and distortions. And the journal is a perfect place to house them.

All of which makes a journal sound like a tidy little closet in which we store moments ordained to be significant, memorable. That's not it at all. Your typical day is probably much like mine: riotously dull. Yet even the drabbest day provides more to write about than we could possibly log. This becomes increasingly true once the journal habit sets in, and we realize that the daily writing process has sensitized us — that we have grown more aware of ourselves and our responses to the mundane world — that we are far less likely to view the day as being featureless, forgettable. "I must get that down in my journal" isn't, for committed journal keepers, a resolution to scribble something daily because it's a good exercise in self-discipline; it's a statement charged with eagerness, with the itch to catch a scene or a notion before it gets away.

- It's fascinating looking back over old pages. Who was I then, compared with now? Why, that is, on the night of January 16, 1980, would I choose to go on for nearly a page about a movie I saw as a kid that scared the pants off me? Or to note the next night only that, "The potatoes I cooked in the coals of my woodstove emerged looking like the remains of martyred Christians"? Here on the 12th of February is a resolution never to leave "this stony land," elsewhere brief dissertations on snoring, modern jazz, trout. There are snatches of overheard conversations, interesting quotes I stumbled across, bits of verse, notes on the seasons, the wildlife:

    3/5: A late-night hike. From beyond the hill on the beaver pond the clattering raucous honk of Canada geese, and in moments they are up above me, flying across the moon, their gray bellies and underwings blending with the night until, disembodied now, they are only the mounting, hungry-harsh song of spring . . .

    Predictions ("the well will go dry by July"), general trivia, e.g., "Bob makes the kind of martinis Spitfire pilots used to drink before they wobbled into the night sky to get shot down by sober Germans.''

A bit of philosophizing:

I just watched a buckwheat fly expire, and it came to mind that maybe death isn't so mysterious a thing after all. The fly had come to its dying time and had done what it was supposed to do on this Tuesday in early November, along with so many of its fellows.

I've wished these pesky insects dead a thousand times and have tried all fall to hurry them to it with chemicals and swatting. But I got to watching this one fly tonight, and it was worth it having him around for what he took me to reconsidering. The fly was buzzing above my little table, just within the arc of light from the lantern. And he went around and around in the same slow circle, as if he was preoccupied with something pretty deep, the way a person will wear a path in a carpet working out a problem. Then, when he was maybe two feet over my coffee cup, he stopped. I don't mean he stopped *circling*; I mean he stopped *living*, cashed in his chips and plopped directly into my coffee and floated there like a little raisin. There is nothing remarkable about this in itself. It's somewhat remarkable at this time of year to get through a meal without at least one fly crash-landing in it. While neither Emily Post nor Miss Manners covers this exigency, the local propriety seems tasteful enough: you fish the thing out of your food as daintily as possible and flick it onto the floor. But when I did that tonight, I saw dead flies all around me! I'd swept only yesterday, so these fellows had to have died sometime this evening, maybe a hundred of them or more, all at about the same time.

Which is what put me to thinking that what's born at a certain time is just as naturally going to die at a certain time, no matter what church he goes to or how many laps he can do in the pool; and that this part of life's business is no more mysterious than growing whiskers. Maybe that fly was a Methuselah, but I doubt it. The chances are he was standard issue and nothing special, no older or smarter than any of the others lying dead on my cabin floor. I don't know what's pushed us so far off from our natural participation in this cycle, what makes us think we're significantly different from a buckwheat fly and not wired up to last just so long and no longer. Dying wouldn't be nearly as confusing or embarrassing if we stopped to figure that most of the people who were hatched out on a Tuesday in November of a certain year should be getting ready to make a few preoccupied circles and simply stop buzzing — and even more important, that we shouldn't waste our time trying to buzz any louder or fancier than all the others in the bunch. It all comes down, finally, to falling and, I hope, being good and dead before we hit.

An account of a nocturnal visit:

> I'm bounded in by beauty. It even seeks me out in sleep. The other morning at about four I wakened to a racket just beneath me in the kitchen. A rat, I thought, and it's into the cake I bought at the school bake sale. I grabbed the flashlight and crept across the loft floor, more curious than determined. Hanging head and shoulders over the edge, I played the beam toward the noise. It wasn't on the counter by the cake, however; it was in the middle of the room, where my garbage bag had become an animate thing, leaping and scuttling about the kitchen.
>
> A rat large and brash enough to cause all that commotion isn't the kind to run away from an argument, so I figured on shooting the entire affair, and never mind what the birdshot did to the floor. But just then the bag suddenly stilled and from a hole in its side emerged an exquisite little ermine, pure white except for the half-inch of black at the tip of its tail. It sat up and gazed unblinkingly into the light. I turned it off — the moon was bright, and I was struck with the urge to let the animal see me too — but when I did, it slipped back into the bag, and soon it was bouncing wildly around the room again. After a couple of minutes it stopped and the little fellow exited, vanishing under the stove and out the hole for the water pipe.
>
> I was delighted by the visit. The next day I looked up *ermine* in an encyclopedia and discovered that my guest had been a "least weasel," the smallest wild carnivore in North America and by its size, a female. That's all an ermine is — a weasel that turns white in winter. My entire anatomy does the same thing but without any increase in value. For the last couple of nights I've put out a bit of food before bed, but she hasn't returned.

For better or worse, that's a younger me in there, a fellow I can rediscover simply by paging through an old notebook. Figuratively, words in a journal turn time into clear water. You can see down through it to what was.

Writing to remember. . . . A friend and mentor, Jimmy Britton, concludes a memoir that looks back with the aid of journal entries to a harrowing incident in World War Two: "Only very rarely did I find my eighty-year-old self at odds with—that is to say puzzled by, or critical of, or hostile to—the goings on in the life of that thirty-two-year-old. It seems to me I liked what he liked and am interested in what interested him; and have nothing but regret that I can no longer do all that he did or feel all that he felt.'' An elegantly simple summing up of why anyone should be keeping a journal.

Furthermore, consider that we tend to write more reasonably than we act. Writing, perhaps because of its more temperate pace, seems to check the purely impulsive, to beat back the irrational. It's downright difficult to misbehave on paper for very long; I've tried and it was exhausting. Only on paper have I discovered that I am not simply the sum of my eccentricities, quirks, cranky spells—the irritating, unlovable qualities I manifest from time to time and long thought defined my nature. No amount of writing will ever provide an answer to the great Oedipal question, Who am I? But it can bring us an inch or so closer to knowing.

I said above that a journal is, ideally, unself-conscious. It can and should include anything you feel like jotting, no matter how silly or unlikely it might strike somebody else. A journal is, to quote Henry David Thoreau, ''of myself, for myself.'' But it's eventually for others too: your loved ones, your survivors. Ironically, the best way to be remembered through the pages of your journal is to avoid trying to record portents, profundities, immortal lines generally. Much of what Thoreau entered in his journal dealt with piddling matters. The enduring popular esteem of his journals has much to do with what his writings let us know of the man himself. Unless you're foolish enough to shrug off my persuasions about journal keeping, your words will preserve your presence in the family for generations to come.

As Rhoda Maxwell, teacher and mother, puts it, ''We treasure photographs of people important to our personal history, but as those silent faces stare back, I wonder what they thought and felt. If they had kept a journal . . . I would have some sense of what has helped to shape my experiences, my role in history. For that reason, I now keep a journal, not for an unknown, unseen audience, but for me—a part of me that will be accessible to my family's future generations.''

- It works the other way too: young people learn to respect writing and to know it as a central aspect of life by living in a home where parents and siblings frequently write. Conversely, children learn nothing about writing in a home where little writing occurs. For that matter, nearly every act of writing described in this book has a secondary motive: that of making it a highly *visible* family activity. It's a fact that literacy not only begins at home; the degree to which literate activities are practiced there determines young people's lifelong sensibilities about them.

TIPS FOR JOURNAL WRITERS

- When you write in your journal should be whatever time of day is most convenient and gratifying. Lunch hour? Just before bedtime? First thing in the morning? Up to you. It won't take long for you to discover when the best stuff tends to flow from your pen — when you feel most eager to jot. I do think it's important to fix a time and stick to it, come hell or high water. For at least a month, write for fifteen to twenty minutes a day at exactly the same time. No interruptions, diversions, changes in schedule allowed. Writers are athletes of a sort, and you're in training.

- Should you impose this regimen on other family members? Very gently, if at all. It's hard to imagine a more pleasant family ritual than daily journal writing sessions with everyone engaged. But it isn't realistic. Plenty of faithful, years-long journal keepers write only once or twice a week, and it's a rare one who doesn't let the thing lapse for long stretches. Furthermore, journal writing isn't for everyone a twenty-minute occasion. I've often written only a sentence or two on a given day, but just as often I've gone on for four or five pages nonstop.

- Should very young children be expected to keep a journal? Not in the conventional sense. Young children shouldn't be expected to do much of anything routinely; what habits youngsters develop are mostly in the satisfaction of sensual pleasures. But kids are notoriously imitative, and I'd encourage the copy-cat instinct. Make sure that they have their own collection of magic markers and felt-tip and ballpoint pens in favorite colors, along with plenty of crayons and pencils. I recommend providing loose sheets of sturdy paper rather than pages already bound in a notebook. It's easy enough to collect a child's efforts, punch holes in the sheets, and insert them in a loose-leaf binder. An alternative is to store them in an accordion folder, in order but loose. (This allows for the use of large construction paper.) Encourage them to spell out JOURNAL in bright letters on its cover, and make a fuss about assigning a secure, private place for it, away from snooping siblings but accessible to its owner. I'd advise against pushing youngsters to write. It could sour them. Instead, an occasional, "I'm going to write in my journal. Want to write in yours too?" makes it the child's choice rather than that of an authority figure. Two more pointers: It's important that a young child's journal-keeping efforts be highly praised. It's equally important that you refer to it as his or her *journal*; it's one of those words with strongly positive, grown-up connotations.

- Journals afford a place for private writing—the kind we'd be reluctant to have others read, even family members. I don't mean gush of the Dear Diary ilk; I'm talking about half-formed notions, fears, dreams, wishes, plans for the future, critical comments about others, confessional passages—randomly personal stuff that, bodied into written words, might compromise or embarrass its author or somebody else. So it's extremely important to establish from the outset that you won't pry into anyone's journal and that you expect the same of every family member. (It wouldn't be at all important were it not that humans are the nosiest animals on earth.)

- At least once a week plan a journal read-around. There are no rules to guide this practice beyond everyone's listening attentively to whatever the reader has chosen to share and nobody's being critical of subject matter, style, and most especially mechanical errors. For that matter, families should make an enduring habit of weekly readings-aloud of anything, journal extracts to be included, but just as appropriately five minutes' worth of Charles Dickens or Garrison Keillor, a letter written by an ancestor or a current family member, an editorial, brief article, poem, song lyric, short-short story—whatever amuses, engages, instructs. Do encourage pre-readers to participate. *Three-year-olds don't know that they can't read and write.* So ask them to read the stories they make with cryptic crayon scrawls, even if you can't, and be sure to applaud the results.

- Visits away from home, vacation trips, camp, a weekend with a friend or relative, extra long drives—these aren't occasions for leaving the journal home but for bringing it along. Indeed, one way to keep kids from being utterly bored and eventually fractious on a trip is to charge them with keeping a travel journal—something between a nautical log, a scrapbook, and a personalized travelogue-chronicle of the journey. We often did this and then held nightly readings. What never ceased to interest me is how each of us perceived the day so differently that it seemed we had been on separate ventures. (A somewhat Hitlerian acquaintance became so taken with the travel journal idea that he *demanded* a daily accounting on paper. Those who failed to comply went without dessert.) A related keep-them-occupied-on-a-trip idea comes from Ann, my wife. While it doesn't amount to journaling in a specific sense, it's a *composing* activity ideal for long auto trips. When she and her four young children took their annual Wisconsin to New York State trips, the kids were provided with stacks of old magazines, blunt-bladed scissors, paste, crayons, and individual notebooks. The project involved writing stories or accounts of the trip, illustrated with clipped-out pictures.

TYPES OF JOURNALS

The family journal almost certainly didn't originate with me, although I'd never heard of one when I wrote the idea up a few years back. Of all the suggested engagements with writing described in this book, the family journal is the one I most wish we'd happened on when the kids were young. It's simple enough: somewhere in prominent and convenient display, put a journal, open and inviting, a clutch of pens nearby. I'd jot something in passing, wouldn't you? I've talked about developing writing *habits, practices, rituals.* Here, in the family journal, is the potential for a powerful, wonderfully rich *tradition* to be passed down from generation to generation.

Consider the possibilities from a geometric perspective alone: each of your children maintains a family journal with his or her spouse and children. They in turn do the same, as does each of their children. Within three generations the *Jones Family Journals* would fill a small library, collectively one of the richest gatherings of writing by and about any family in history. But I don't suggest such an undertaking in the hope that you'll break into the *Guinness Book of World Records;* it's the immediate richness of the family journal that should draw people to it.

Arlene Mulligan, a devoted family journal keeper, comments, "We began the journal in April. Memorial Day is when we began journal #2 because #1 was full to the brim. . . . We found it a good place to play with scraps of life. No deadlines, no pressure to perform — an extension of good talk, but distinctly different." In her letter to me she went on to say that when friends visit, they rush for the journal "to catch up on what's been going on here." Still later Mulligan shared a notion well worth repeating: in the process of writing to a Canadian relative whom she had seen only once over many years, she realized that she couldn't possibly summarize her family's everyday life at home. So she included some random family journal entries. ("I don't think anything could have convinced Sharron of what life in S. California is really like better than the journal entry about getting a possum out from under my bed.") The near-immediate result was "as a Christmas present, a series of journal entries to add to our collection. Trading and adding to family journals—like swapping baseball cards but better!" At last report the exchange continues, with contributions from relations who had previously sent only an occasional greeting card or nothing at all.

- The round-robin journal will work only if every last contributor cooperates, in most families a circumstance that at best can only be approached, never achieved. There's always Uncle Gene out in Seattle, who doesn't get around to mailing Christmas cards until Memorial Day, and Muriel's nasty husband Claude, who would leap at the chance to fill pages with snide remarks about what everybody else writes. I'd suggest your launching a circulating journal anyhow, on a trial basis at least. Select in advance a smallish group of compatible relatives and close family friends, win their promise of cooperation beforehand, make some initial entries yourselves, and mail it off with a covering letter requesting that the first recipient(s) make an entry within two to three days, then mail it on to the next name on the letter. One family I'm familiar with has participated in this kind of journaling for nearly a dozen years. Their network includes ten contributing households. Together they have filled twenty-one notebooks. At least three participants had not yet been born when the round-robin began. Nice idea, the kind I love to hear about.
- Another family journal habitue from Eau Claire, Wisconsin, told me about her clan's longstanding custom, the camp journal. It's the nearly sacred obligation of whoever spends time at the family's deep-woods retreat to put aside time for writing in the journal that has occupied the same familiar place there for fifteen years.
- Jean Altendorf, from Lisle, Illinois, offers this idea, which brings to mind a dozen possible variations: "When my mother went to Hawaii, the rest of us spent a lot of time at my folks' house looking after my elderly father. As a way to keep her up on the news we kept a daily journal. She loved reading it on her return."
- Roger Shuy, a professor of linguistics at Georgetown University, shared with me a manuscript he'd written about a significant stretch of journal-keeping from his youth. *Pop and the Sports Book* was meant as a nostalgic tribute to his father, but also as a reflection about how writing inspired and sustained by a parent leads to life-long literate practices.

One day in the spring of 1941, when I was ten years old, Pop gave me a very odd present—a small green book that he had purchased at the local five and ten cent store. The cover was printed "The Scribble-In

Book, Trademark.'' I opened it at once and found it completely blank. ''It's for you to write in,'' he told me. ''What do I write?'' ''Whatever you want.''

After decorating the inside cover with a drawing of the American flag, Roger printed ''Baseball,'' ''Football,'' and ''Basketball,'' and beneath added two ''Yea's.''

This was to be a *sports book*. Why a sports book? What else would a ten-year-old boy think of when his father's picture hung on the walls of Kenmore High School as captain of the basketball team, track star, swimmer, and outstanding left fielder?

With some gentle nudging from his invalided father, Roger became a chronicler of the uneven fortunes of the Cleveland Indians, his father's as well as his own favorite team. For three years he maintained his sports book (which could also be classified as a *specialized* or *theme-specific* journal), sometimes embellishing his entries with cartoons, another talent awakened by his dad.

Occasionally, his father would insert an entry, too. *The Sports Book* became a forum for opinions, speculations, predictions. Although the journal dealt specifically with the Indians, it was, in retrospect, about profounder matters: ''I think my father was telling me that I could actually create a world that I liked or wanted or enjoyed by guessing at what the end of the season would be like.''

When I wrote to Roger thanking him for sharing his work with me, I commented, ''Your relationship with your father is a wonderful proof of the bonding writing provides. All the 'reach out and touch someone' and 'when you care enough to send the very best . . .' hoopla outshouts the simple fact that writing belongs at the center of and helps define the very concept of family.'' Although he doesn't say so in his manuscript, it's clear to me from reading *Pop and the Sports Book* that Roger Shuy's early journal turned out to be the most important book in his life.

- Roger Shuy's wife, Jana Staton, is widely known for her work with dialogue journals. In fact, she has launched a study of families that use journals as a way of communicating between parents and children. Dialogue journals, as the term suggests, are a form of interactive writing, an ongoing back-and-forth, sometimes about matters that would never otherwise get aired.
- A young parent I recently spoke with told me that she and her twelve-year-

old agreed years back to reduce family tensions by writing out their side of any thorny issue that crops up, and then dialoguing on paper until the matter is resolved. "It doesn't always work," she said, "but it usually does cut back on misunderstandings. We don't just write about the particulars of a disagreement; we also deal with how we *feel*. I confess I have a hard time saying out loud, 'I hurt,' but I don't have any trouble writing about it. Neither does she." (This dialogue journal entry by another young mother writing to her ten-year-old daughter after a misunderstanding offers perfect proof of how we can *write* what we often cannot *say:* "I wish it was as possible to yell 'love' as it is possible to yell 'anger.' ")

- An article in the *Journal for the Education of the Gifted* discusses a five-year-old's keeping a dialogue journal with her father. Like Roger Shuy's father, Marie's had given her a notebook and asked that she write in it whatever she wished. On page 31 is one of her early efforts, along with her father's response and a typed transcript. The article observes that Marie's drawing and writing both refined as the journaling went on, perhaps because her father avoided correction and criticism. Furthermore, she obviously enjoyed the exchanges and demanded prompt responses from her father. In light of why you're reading this book, consider this observation:

> . . . her father felt that these demands were helpful both for Marie's developing literacy abilities and for their mutual communication. He found that although he couldn't save Marie's oral communication without audio-taping, he could easily save her written communication in the dialogue journal. The archival nature of dialogue writing was an added advantage. . . . since this communication remained as a family keepsake.

Nioka Houston from Craftsbury, Vermont writes about her participation in what she labels a "communal journal writing project":

> My son [Jon], my daughter [Megan], and I would, on the same page, make a journal entry. The only rule. . . was that they had to pertain to music or piano. On Friday we would give the journal to the piano teacher, Mary Anthony Cox Rowell. . . . She would read the journal in airports during her weekly commute [to New York City] and make responses.

Pages 32 and 33 contain two pages from the communal journal. As you can see, while the subject is indeed music, the piano, it's the wonderfully relaxed intimacy of these exchanges that holds the project together.

- Have you ever thought about paying a youngster to write? While that may sound like the very kind of bribery you and every other right-minded parent should oppose, think again: Writers get paid to write, don't they? And aren't we attempting to get family members old and young to perceive themselves as writers? Furthermore, you probably pay your kids to perform other duties, chores, routines. (Maybe you don't, but you should.) Toby Fulwiler, a friend and college professor well-known for his contributions to the teaching of writing, and Laura, his wife, came up with the notion that to induce their eleven-year-old daughter into the habit of regular writing, they'd make her a deal she couldn't possibly refuse: a half-hour daily at the word processor, 15 minutes to be spent practicing typing, the other 15 minutes to be devoted to writing about something that happened in her day. Both parents would respond to Anna's entries. The incentive was money—a raise in allowance from two to four dollars a week. (Had my father thought to offer me a deal like that I'd have written the Great American Novel before I was sixteen.) Here are a couple of entries, along with responses:

  Monday, 10/14
  Today in Mr. Swierk's class we went into the darkroom. Mr. Swierk had a black light bulb. When he turned off all the lights except the black one everyones white clothes showed up like they were floresent. You couldn't tell the difference between the red and the blue, it was weird!

  Thanks for telling me this, Annie. Could you explain to me *why* the black light bulb made this happen? Or if you couldn't, maybe you can ask Mr. Swierk—because I don't really understand how you can even have such a thing as "black light"—isn't "light" light? Why doesn't a black bulb make everything even more black than it already is? Dad
  Thursday, 10/17
  After school today Susan came over, we painted our bakers clay models of our country. Megan said the mountains, which were painted brown, looked like "poop"! I hope Mr. Earley doesn't think so. Tonight I still have to spray enamel on them, to make them look shiny.

  Dad, I'm sorry, but I forgot to ask Mr. Swierk about the lightbulb.

Sample of Marie and her Father's Dialogue Journal Writing

Your unicorn is very nice. What is
your unicorn's name?

Typed transcription of Marie's (age 5 years 10 months) and her
father's dialogue journal writing:

Marie: iike (picture) UNicoRN (*The Last Unicorn* was one of
        Marie's favorite films)
             tHE LASt
Marie's father: Your unicorn is very nice. What is
             your unicorn's name?
Marie: UNiCORN

✻ Megan, that is one reason why I suggested you play the easy pieces in the Rose Book just once, so you get used to playing a [improvement. For a young man, 8 years old you are doing a FANTASTIC job.] piece of music just like you read a

Megan- you've enjoyed piano this vacation. I've enjoyed listening to you play out of the ✻ book: out of Sound of Music + little band books from Betsy. You ought to play for fun more often. I think vacation gives us time to unwind + do these things. Right or half right?

Curiosity -

Joe, that really is a lovely idea! I used to have some special friends when I was in Paris whom I enjoyed having around when I practised -

Mom I Love to watch you watch me practice. Megan do you ever think about quwiting piano? (I have alot)
M.A. I have been thinking about some stuff that I want to ask you in my other entres.

I'll be looking forward to it.

~~I have a lot~~ Sometimes I think about quiting. One time when I was in 2nd grade I seriously said to mom, "I want to quit piano." Mom said, "I won't let you quit piano," I'm glad I didn't, now, I don't think about quiting anymore.

I never felt like I could afford to say that to my mother, Mom said because since I had asked her to teach me, she was just doing what I asked. So

your right, mom. I agree. Both of us need a cushion!!!

I would complain to my friends instead!!!

When you are growing,
Megan it feels hard. Now think
back to what was hard a year ago.
Megan Houston is present. Go back and play

Actually, I sort of like easy some of that
music better. I think. Well, at least you'll be
its easy to play. But I like amazed how
the sound of hard music sounds comfortable
hard but also sounds accomplishing it will seem!
And to think, back, back,
back, I did finger exercises
for this! I use to hate
those sor much!!! They did
get boring after a while,
you have to admit. One time
I did them at school so but, of course!
I'd have more time to my
self.

Mom and Meg Guess what,
do you have Joe - it
any idea what means putting
procrastination something off
means Meg was as long as
telling me to you can
that I had possibly get
to tell her away with
what it. Some
procrastinaation times I
means. about starting procrastinate to do something that is hard. And then the funniest
thing will happen: I just get tired of
putting the thing off and I start doing it.

Dear Annie, this is getting ridiculous, isn't it: here we are sitting around at midnight talking to you on the computer—why don't we just go up and whisper in your ear? Well, thanks for answering my question about landforms on your island. Remember, I'm still wondering about that black "light" you wrote about on Monday. Dad

Clearly enough, Toby and Laura Fulwiler's ploy isn't just a way to get a child interested in schoolwork. It's also a means for keeping in touch in an age where touching and keeping are virtual lost arts. Through this computer-facilitated dialogue journal, Annie's parents demonstrate their interest in what their daughter is learning, and also in Annie herself. Another plus is that she's learning how to type. All for an extra two bucks a week.

FIELD NOTES

Watching and *writing*—there are occasions when these should become inseparable activities. How often I've contented myself with passive, half-focused observation only to discover an hour or a year later that I'd forgotten the essence of what I'd viewed, failed to understand and learn from it. Watching and writing can amount to a process called field noting. If it's introduced as a pastime early in young people's lives and encouraged over time, it will become a powerful technique for learning about *anything.* It's never too late to begin watching and writing and learning, however. Additionally, field noting can become a pleasant family activity, falling somewhere between sketching and journal keeping.

I've offered on page 36 a completed version of one possible page format for field noting. It would be useful to make up a similar form in multiple copies, provide folders with appropriate name labels, put together an expedition of entomologist/botanist/ornithologist/ichthyologist colleagues, young or old, and strike out for woods, fields, or even the back yard.

This format represents one of many possible approaches to field noting. I like it because, as you can see, it invites subjective responses as well as less personalized description. We tend to think in metaphors—to make our most powerful connections with and through them—and therefore it seems important to invite a jotting down of whatever unaccountable images come to mind. Where does the writer—in this case a young teenager—go from here? It may not matter. What seems clear from this example is that through this form of observing, discovey takes place; she notices things—not only about the apple blossom under scrutiny but also the quality of light, mood, the sensibilities to which she awakens. Her notes, that is, have already taken the writer well beyond the stated subject.

On pages 37 and 38, a much younger writer takes notes on a botany project. Although it was conducted at school, this is precisely the type of close-up watching and writing that can and should happen at home, too. It doesn't have to involve seeds; this engrossing activity could as readily involve a terrarium, an ant colony, a bird feeder (or nesting site), a spider web—preferably any *natural* process going on under our noses and easy to observe. Like any good field noter, this writer has incorporated drawings, including a cover featuring himself, the setting, and the details of his project.

This last example of field noting is more free-form than the preceding ones. Still, it is a *form* of capturing, learning—on-the-spot notes cast in present tense. The life in them keeps, doesn't it? the colors, the wind, the immediacy?

Feb. 2—A cold, blowy Sunday, the snow dry and surging over the black roads like roiled surf. A hawk hangs on the wind, finding in its invisibility a perfect equilibrium, driving into it only enough to go nowhere, to stay, thoughtless about the intricate ways of its wings, the tips prehensile, fingering the air's complicated chords. Lovely, black against the dirty white sky, and when the wind surprises it—holds its gusting breath—the bird drops, then banks and rises, and its undersides are dark and mottled except for the bright chevrons which run the wings' length, their color more buoyant than the air's, light enough to lift a hawk.

Then down, folding, nearly to the ground, and pausing, the thought in the wings, not the animal. Up now, the prey moving, still oblivious to the low-hanging hawk no more than fifteen feet from the ground. The wind takes the bird, the bird, the wind. It shunts toward us watching in the car, riding sideways with the wind to the near edge of the bare field, and four quick wingbeats now to earth. No more than four or five seconds, then up, the legs extended now, both claws clutched, the dying little prey between, a mouse most likely. The hawk flaps off, this time with the wind and burdened and ungainly, settles on a fence post and begins its dinner.

Now, the sun brighter although lower, the girl in the field, a long flat. Much too cold to be riding, but she is at the trot, a red jacket, a bay horse, a Morgan type. Around at the trot flat-saddled in foot-deep snow, the snow going blue, the wind and the trot enough to make the horse's mane fly out. And around she goes, sitting well, the red coat smart against the bay, the blue-white flat; then into a canter, the girl's hair streaming out around her face, then behind. There is no path, no track, just snow. It is good to see;

FIELD NOTES [ON] AN APPLE BLOSSOM

March 18
9:11 pm
backyard
(looking from
window)

PHYSICAL DESCRIPTION
Two white dainty
blossoms with a touch
of pink at the edges
and a pale yellow
center. Green leaves
protect. Shy and
slightly wilted.

METAPHORS
→ · popcorn (explosion of white)
→ · fireworks (at night)
→ · lace (daintiness)

ENVIRONMENT / SURROUNDINGS:
night time; no wind: still
light from my room makes spotlight
compared to others — same
elements (petals / leaves) as
other groups of blossoms but
each has unique structure.
alone at the tip of a branch

PERSONAL FEELINGS:
my mood is calm although I
am tired and under stress
from school & homework.
Looking at the group of blossoms
gives me a sense of tranquility.
It reminds me that Spring is
coming. I take advantage of
their natural beauty (color,
femininity, etc) because I know
they will soon begin to
fall off. It is hard to believe
that in a couple months an
apple will take their place.

1.

(I think it will take 10 days
until it grows and what I did
is get some soil in a cup and I
watered it and it grew).

2.

March 4 1988

(No Plants today)

I like her from a hundred yards away, a young girl trudging against the wind and her sense of the cold out to the barn to do what she senses will be right and eventually grand. She rides face on into the cold; privately she revels in it. You couldn't otherwise last this long out on a flat late in the afternoon with the temperature maybe five or so, around and around, taking it in, turning it into something so privately exhilarating that no matter what you figured, she could look right down her nose at you in a good way because you'd be thinking a wrong and too-meager thing.

March 7, 1988

It Sil is not gon
but it is ok waf me
me and teChr put
in sum noe seed

(It still is not growing but it
is ok with me. Me and teacher
put in some new seed).

4.

March 9 1988

Myplant is not gowing
ol it is der is sot and
the cup.

(My plant is not growing. All
that is there is soil and the
cup).

5.

March 14 1988.

my plants are goen
and i like it kus
i have wated for
it to groe.

(My plants are growing, and I
like it because I have waited for it
to grow).

JOURNAL AS CONFIDANT

A family friend volunteered for this book a journal she had kept during the
latter stages of her husband's terminal illness. In the note that accompanied
the thick packet of handwritten pages she said, "From whatever vantage point
you read this journal, it functioned as a living thing for me."

I expected a psychic melt-down. What I found instead were the requisite props of sanity. In the approximately 80 pages was not one self-pitying line, no breast-beating, nothing darkly fatalistic. It isn't that Judy's entries are marked by self-imposed restraints—that even in her own journal she has maintained a privacy so complete as to keep life (and impending death) from its pages. Halfway through a third reading it struck me that her phrase for the journal, "a living thing," wasn't tossed off; that she meant it exactly. The "thing" is busy with the kind of talk we all seek audience for, especially in times of stress—talk we can direct at an empty yet sympathetic page, knowing that we won't have to listen to well-intended but useless platitudes in response.

She frets about their children, confesses to a day-long chocolate-eating binge, lays out a set of resolutions about the future, details the sounds and smells of a cross-town bus ride (she is away from home with her husband while he receives treatment at a specialized medical facility), worries about her work, expresses anger (again and again) about her husband's misery, records an elevator ride with a corpse, tallies how much the time away from her job has cost, goes over what lies ahead when they return home—the routine, the stuff that makes us necessary, requires our presence, keeps us from flying off the edge of the world.

It is ever remarkable to me how much we can know of the writer from a journal—how impossible it is to maintain a false identity for more than a page or two, to lie to "a living thing." This is discoverable for the writer too, in going over pages distanced from the present by as little as a week. It would be impossible to single out three or four of these entries to exemplify what I mean. There is nothing startling or moving about any one or a dozen, as their author would surely agree. In a way, that is what is most remarkable about this journal, about any mundane ledger. They keep us honest, keep us talking, keep us from flying off the edge. I can't think of a better way to come upon yourself than by reading through a reach of your own past journal entries. Nor can I think of a much better way to allow others to do the same.

CHAPTER THREE

Letters

An old saying goes that there is a moment in every day that the Devil cannot find. I mostly choose to fill that moment with letter writing. Ask anyone who puts words to paper more or less regularly; you'll find that writers of any age develop a favorite medium, a form of expression that's especially enjoyable, tonic, even therapeutic. Years ago I settled on letter writing. Since then I've countlessly observed that if a person discovers in a lifetime two or three trusted correspondents, he or she is truly blessed.

Using a letter to one of my closest correspondents as evidence, I earlier (p. 11) observed that we often discover what to write about by writing. I meant that deeply; it isn't one of those trite little homilies writers toss off. I think this is what most fires the near-daily urge to dash off a letter: the half-conscious sense that something totally unanticipated is bound to emerge—even that on occasion what comes out will be effortlessly lovely prose. I never work at personal letters; what comes comes. It occurred to me not long back that I wouldn't mind being judged as a writer or a human on the strength of all those letters. Then it came to mind that ultimately I *will* be so judged—that much of this stuff will eventually find its way into my kids' hands, giving rise to revelations, new perspectives about their father, good ones, I hope.

When I write without fixed purpose to another, with no more intent, say, than to amuse or reflect or fulfill an obligation, or even and especially to put off work, I often jot my way into fascinating places. Furthermore, although I have always found focused, fairly formal writing such as what you're reading terribly difficult to the point where I gladly run from it, I most often start the day itching to write to a friend.

A GATHERING OF LETTERS

Rather than launch into a string of encouragements about why you too should be writing letters regularly, let me offer these examples, chiefly for your amusement and not to serve as models, and additionally this admonishment: don't be guided by anything you think you know about the fine art of letter writing, the Victorian conventions that long governed the form, or what you think your correspondents expect you to say. I love letter writing because, aside from my journal, it's the only place I can say whatever comes to mind in the comfortable knowledge that the reader will somehow understand. (For that matter, my letters and journal entries are mostly indistinguishable from one another. This happens quite naturally as trusting relationships between correspondents develop.)

I hope that these examples, some complete letters, some excerpts, will also serve somewhat as illustrations in an anatomy text do—that you'll see in them what's going on beneath the surface; how a mind empty of thought can be galvanized by the faintest glimmer of a subject; how writing may either be the *outcome* of thought or thought actually forming on the page, at the moment of being. If we could chart how this first letter, for instance, finds its way in a page and a half from an extreme of whimsy to a doomsday vision, we would in effect be laying bare the workings of the unconscious, tracking the involuntary assembly of irrational matter into meaning.

These are the cars I have owned in the order of my owning them, in the order that God ordained our coming together, an order that was Holy and Right and Beautiful, like the Stations of the Cross.

A '38 Buick convertible with a rumbleseat and a Fireball eight
A '32 Packard Victoria with cut-glass bud vases and a 7-foot hood
A '38 Packard sedan whose clutch my girlfriend blew out
A '40 Plymouth 2-door with the shift right up there on the wheel
A '42 Nash coupe, black and utterly uninteresting
A '47 Cadillac convertible, long and sexy as a serious kiss
A '35 Dodge thronging with old ladies' ghosts
A '51 Morris wagon, tiny and loathesome
A '56 Volkswagen the color of embarrassment and bad dawns
A '50 MG we souped up so hot it would barely run on gasoline
A '62 Volvo 544, eye-shadow blue and indomitable
A '62 Rambler sedan nobody had ever made love in
A '48 Buick convertible that honest-to-God liked me
A '65 Ford Galaxy in which I destroyed a Kharman Ghia, a privet hedge, and finally my relative innocence
A '66 Ford Country Squire with the heart of a Clydesdale
A '68 Ford Country Squire clean enough to take to bed

A '70 Chevy wagon as drab as a submarine's insides
A '72 Audi so corrupt I still can't bear talking about it
An '82 Rabbit that helped me discover where my sciatic nerve is.

There are in this world countless people with whom I share a birthday, perhaps half a hundred men alive with my name, maybe even one whose children are named as mine are. Nowhere, though, in the history of this planet has another mortal ever owned cars in the same order and color and vintage as these. So hard it is, especially in these times, to find about oneself an estimable uniqueness of the kind you can trot out for others to see. It just now occurs to me as I look back over this list that it amounts to my having erected a hall of fame and being its sole inductee. You can see, too, how downright sensible it would be to mail such a list to a therapist instead of sitting around some genuine-wood-grain formica waiting room reading back issues of *People.* All a psychologist would have to do is run the thing through a computer and it would sum you up and boil you down so you and all your problems would fit on one side of a bubblegum card.

Shucks, you could even run for office on the strength of such a list. "Here," you'd say to voters, "look at all that star-spangled iron—Packards, Buicks, a Caddy for God's sake, and all them big old wagons right at a time when who knows how many lily-livered, mealy-mouth folks was worryin' about the country going plumb to hell and trottin' out and buyin' a mess of sissy cars so small you could practically stick 'em right in the damn oven! And now you look at what my opponent here was drivin' back then. Guess you know who had faith in this here nation and who was runnin' scared."

You know what just struck me I got to do? Get every last one of those cars chiseled on my tombstone, right under that good old line from "Hail Mary": "Pray for us sinners now and at the hour of our death, Amen." Knock-out stuff, maybe run it in with the automobiles. Somehow seems to belong there, under that '38 Buick. The first time some greasy-knuckled Catholic kid slides behind the wheel of his very own car, he'd better have some company with a mile more clout than that tinhorn St. Christopher, because he's going to flip that top down never mind it's raining and February and rev that Fireball straight-8 vroom-vroom about a dozen times and grab that ruby-red skull with the fake diamond eye and slam her down into first and maybe three more vrooms and you better have a little Hail Mary on board or what's to stop you from laying it right to the floor and burning your way clear off the edge of the world and tearing a smoky hole in the night, your girlfriend's hair blowing wild and beautiful and wicked and every last little bone shiny white and guaranteed to last just as long as a person would ever want. Oh Lordy. Oh, Lordy, lordy, lordy. Now and at the hour . . .

••••••

Thank you for the lovely letter and especially the poem within it. The latter is tacked on the small piece of wall that has been covered with sheetrock. That should tell you that I cherish it already. The only other things on that wall are a photo of Jon jumping his yellow horse over a fence and beneath that a whimsical line from Lewis Carroll. It was on a waitress's t-shirt in Nag's Head, North Carolina, an unpretentious and charming quote printed in black against a yellow background. It said " 'Now that we've seen each other,' said the unicorn, 'I'll believe in you if you believe in me.' "

Tonight you'll sit down together to a tasty supper, after which you will amuse yourselves in enviable ways. I'll have most of a package of frozen lima beans and sit in the dark because I've let myself run out of gasoline for the Coleman again. What beans I don't finish I'll throw out the door. That isn't as messy and irresponsible as it sounds. Everything I throw out the door up here is gone by morning. If I threw out an old pair of boots, a boot-eating denizen of these woods would smell them and swing by to carry them off. It is practically sure-fire. Chicken bones, stale bread, margarine wrappers — it's all gone by morning. Tomorrow night I am going to throw out all the unpaid bills. Somewhere nearby is an animal who'll eat them.

I don't think I've written to you since my son Jon's wedding last weekend. The kids referred to the priest who was to marry them as Father Willie, which led me to wrong conclusions. Willie gave me a shot right in the heart. He made an observation I've written and talked about a hundred times. He said, "You know, this society we live in is remarkably articulate. We have developed splendid dialects for dealing with science and technology and economics and even the arts. But we don't have many ways to talk about love. We use it, for example, mostly as a noun. We use it to label things. I don't think it should be used that way. It works much better as a participle."

He was a skinny, quite homely fifty-ish fellow and tipped a bit to the left from I guess a bad back. He fumbled twice with his robes, once to get a handkerchief to blow his large beak of a nose and once to put it back again. It interrupted and preoccupied him unduly. But when he picked up again on what he was saying, he simply got better and better. I'm not easy to impress, but he never got maudlin or saccharine, and when he swung onto Margaret and Jon he said to his congregation, "I've performed 536 weddings, and mostly you know pretty quickly how you feel about the couple, whether you really like them or not. And I want to tell you that I'm crazy about these two young people." And he stepped from behind his lectern with the cross on the front of it and hugged the two of them with a gusto and affection that was honest and packed with joy and hope for them.

••••••

I've just been browsing a book, John Bliebtrau's *The Parable of the Beast*. Perhaps you've come across it in your eclectic way of finding out good stuff; at any rate I'd suggest your looking it up. The first time through it is a series of astonishments, although "embarrassments" would better suit; for he has, in unarguably accurate and dispassionate terms, underscored again and again how we as a species have fought (to our collective and individual misery) the very nature of ourselves—how we have through elaborately concocted denials attempted to erase the memories and messages our cells are imprinted with.

Somewhere in the revised edition of the myth book I comment on cyclical time: how we are designed to repond to tidal, seasonal, solar, and lunar rhythms and how instead we have imposed a linearity to virtually all our measurements—how we put time behind us and measure our own lives serially: past, present, future— a fatalistic perspective, always and inevitably an end mark in mind, a terminal point. Yet I feel the other pull; I always have. Probably everybody does; it is a perennial cause of internal arguments with the self. I mean I participate without conscious intent in the inevitability of sping, I celebrate it always. It is meant, Eliot aside, to be joyful, a reaffirmation of the truth that life does not wind down; it repeats. And it positively pisses me off to discover that each rebirth is for me tinged by the rueful acknowledgment that it is my fortieth or fiftieth spring and that I therefore have one less blossoming to go. I am one pitted constantly against possi- bility, against old wisdoms, the wisdom of trees, say, or wild asters, or damn near anything willing to die and be reborn, to change in tune with the reasonable demands of the very intelligent planet we live on.

There is, according to Bleibtrau (about whom I wrote to you from the cabin years back, it just now occurs), simply no way to outfox the fiddler crab, which in a series of experiments conducted at the Univ. of Illinois some years back, kept faith with the moon. Fiddler crabs turn bright yellow at high tide, then dun at low. Dr. Frank A. Brown, Junior, brought back from the Atlantic tidal waters a mess of the creatures and impounded them in tanks far from the ocean's tidal pull. Yet the fiddlers maintained the color shift, right to the minute. To test his thesis that the crabs were being directed by the moon, he built a set of double tanks, which were insulated against varying atmospheric pressures. The crabs responded by ignoring his efforts, changing colors daily, their transformations timed to the fifty-minute daily change in the high and low measures of the oceans' tides.

When (and most especially why) did we wander away from such cosmic tug- gings? When/why did we elect to paint our doom on calendars, measure it in minutes, lost springs, rituals of aging, celebrations of death? There's more than one way to look at a thing is all I mean; and increasingly I do it ass-backwards. This struck me with particular force today, a crisp and otherwise unnotable Tuesday in October, when I quit work for an hour at three to take the dog and the shotgun for a hike in the strip of woods above the two ponds just down the road. The way was boggy; I knew that few partridges would be walking the bottom. So I kept looking up, figuring to spot one in the hemlocks or the maples. The Brittany bounded along, oblivious to the fact that a year in her age is roughly the equivalent to seven of mine. She harbored no faint anxieties about her mortality; the smell of it all was what mattered. I pulled up next to a waterfall, laid down my shotgun (a prop; I almost never shoot it, miss when I do) and fell immediately to brooding about how beautiful was the light suffusing through the yellows of maple, ash and birch; and how I had consciously avoided a steep slope and stuck to the flat; and how it would take at least half an hour for the pool below the falls to clear now that I'd silted it up from splashing around above it; and how I can't swing a shotgun the way I could a few years back; and finally (after I'd sat down on a rock and gotten into the heavy stuff) how I'd gone and slipped into a terrible notch in life — somewhere between being middle-aged and dead and leaning toward the latter almost in a sense of relief. A partridge flushed about then and the dog got so exercised about that that she jumped into the icy little pool and came out looking like a freckled otter, which was funny as hell to see and took me to laughing and then bang! right back to thinking I wish I'd been a farmer. I don't know what to do about any of this other than fall in love with everything, even fiddler crabs.

•••••••

Yesterday while lying in the bathtub I wondered why John Cheever did not write plays, and when I emerged I read in *Time* that his first play, on PBS, had been a smash. I make nothing of that, nothing at all; it simply seemed an apt enough way to open a letter. I had planned originally to talk to you about this morning instead, when at about 5:30 I began to have serious doubts about the speed of light. I arose at seven, knowing I'd been roundly fooled about it, along with millions of others. Nothing, Frank, travels at 186,000 miles per second, and all it takes is a little quiet thought to figure it out. It is maybe 1200 miles from Utica to Dubuque, and if I lit a match in Utica (I just did, in fact), its flare would get to Iowa about 150 years before I was born. Doesn't make a shred of sense. Further proof is that last week I lit the lantern in the cabin and maybe 10 minutes later walked into the open oven door, skinning my shin. But five or so minutes after that I could see the damn thing practically as clear as day. It took nearly a quarter hour for that light to travel maybe 16 feet. The cabin temperature was nearly zero, and I figure that light doesn't travel as fast when it's cold. Play around with these so called scientific truths and you find out that at least half of them are pure hogwash.

It was so cold that night — I had been away from the place for a few days — that the alarm clock was frozen. I set it on a chair by the fire, no closer than I would place an honored guest, and the face melted so that the hands got pinned to 2:15, probably the most useless time of night. I went to bed disgusted and thought about things I hated venomously. The squirrel woke me at six. I don't know how it gets in and out of the place or why it bothers. I burn my garbage in the stove, and there is nothing in my tiny larder even faintly interesting to squirrels. But it skritches and clatters around like a thing demented and one night crashed into the cedar chest by my bed. Sometimes the cabin seems to take on a life of its own. The mice come out of the oven and eat my soap and frolic in the sink, and the cluster flies, who lie seemingly dead along the windowsills, rise in ghoulish squadrons once the sun sets. I do not know what to make of the tracks just outside my door. Last week I threw out an apple core and the next day it was gone. A set of tracks came out from under a hemlock tree, passed ten feet to the left of the core, halted, looped in an irregular circle, then went to the core and disappeared again under the same hemlock. Whatever it was had feet shaped like bottlecaps but larger, about the size of those little plastic ashtrays you see in McDonald's restaurants, and was longish and narrow and built rather low to the ground. A furrow ran down the middle of the footprints. I am satisfied that the markings were made either by someone wearing ashtrays on his hands and feet and dragging a suitcase behind him or by a crocodile with rounded-off paws. I do not want either of them hanging around the place. Nobody would.

••••••

A long time ago I learned that water sleeps at night, and that if a horse drinks sleeping water, it'll die. That's why a horse always snorts into water after dark, to wake it up.

••••••

When I'm done with this letter, I'm going to sign the back of my driver's license under the little paragraph of consent that lets the state remove my organs and use them in much the good and various ways states use up the outsides of people. The alternative comes down to vanity, I decided just the other night.

"I hereby make an anatomical gift. . ." the contract reads. That is a gentle yet accurate way to put the ceding of one's guts; for three-quarters of its length, in fact, it is a perfectly iambic line. Just beneath it lie choices to be made. My options are to make the ultimate anatomical gift: "any needed organs or parts," or to limit the offering to "the following body parts" (yet here the blank line is only about two inches long; you'd damn near fill it up with "duodenum"). The next line invites still more waffling. "Limitations" is all it says, with the blank following it running a good half-inch longer than the one just above it. Still, that isn't nearly room enough; if "Limitations" isn't an irresistible essay title, I don't know what is. Don't break up any sets, I want to say; do not use my components in frivolous ways. I do not want this once-noble heart ending up in a dissecting tray in some crummy two-year college biology class outside of Buffalo. It is not vanity but rea-sonable sensitivity to shudder at the thought of some vacuous gum-chewing twit giving it an arm's length poke and saying "Yeeeck!" at the top of her unsigned-away lungs.

I would've signed the thing and stuck it back in my wallet before it became so fraught with ambiguity but for the fact that it also calls for the signatures of two witnesses. That's really all I wanted to write to you about—whether you'd be one of them. In exchange I'd sign over to you whatever might strike your fancy, so long as you could squeeze it into the blank after "limitations." (You have a good sense of irony or I wouldn't be asking. On the other hand your penwomanship tilts toward the hieroglyphic, so God only knows what you'd end up with.)

"All of me," that old ballad goes. "Why not take all of me? You took the part that once was my heart, so why not take all of me?" It's even catchier than "I hereby make an anatomical gift. . ." Maybe I'll staple the lyrics to my license and sign the bottom of them instead.

······

When I was little and had to go to bed just when the day had begun to dim into promise, I nearly always played my Emerson table radio with the white plastic case and the soft orange light illuminating the numbers on the dial. I wasn't supposed to play the radio; I was supposed to fall asleep, because if you do that when you're little it is very good for the healthy growth of all your myriad parts excepting maybe the mind.

I turned down the volume so that what sound came out was very faint and mine alone. Then I turned it down some more, so that it was impossible to hear even from a foot or so away. A little wire came out the back of the radio. It was an aerial of sorts. I wound it around my finger, and when I did, the sound would lift just enough for me to hear. As I fell off to sleep, I knew, the wire would work itself loose, so that when my parents came upstairs to bed there would be no forbidden voices whispering from my room.

It was pleasant being an aerial. I used to lie there thinking about how the sounds that issued from the little white box were entirely dependent on me—that I was in those hours more radio than it, picking up programs that came across the night sky and into my room lit only by the dial's glow—that the wire and I continued out into the dark and down the street and across places that were hazy to me then because although I believed them to be I had never seen and are hazy to me still because although I have seen them I less and less believe them to be; and finally to the source of each voice, each sound. Put your ear to me those nights and you could hear whatever program I was tuned to—"Inner Sanctum," "Lights Out," "I Love a Mystery," "The Lux Radio Theatre," "Fibber McGee and Molly."

They're in me still, forms of matter I absorbed back in the forties. Otherwise how could I now hear the creaking door or those great, pealing bells or, perfectly, the voice of Baby Snooks? It isn't memory; I can't get that aspect of my being to do anything I ask it to. It is having been an aerial, drawing those sounds invisibly as gamma rays through my growing bones right into the marrow of me. If I wanted to, I could play a half-hour's worth of Charlie McCarthy right now. Hasn't got a thing to do with remembering.

······

I would like to comment on the fawn I saw this morning, but first to tell you that the big red-tail that hunts the haylot goes one-two-three with his tawny wings, then glides, then again the three beats and the hanging for a hundred feet on the same air I draw at that moment into my sleepy, unflapping body. That was this morning, early. Tonight he again took off from the same field, the hawk, and flew magically through the branches of a maple tree and came out the other side going one-two-three-glide, as if he had been drilled to the beat in a dancing school. (One-two-three-glide, Mrs. Canfield told us in the humid hall above Bryant-Besse Haberdashers on Wall Street a block up from the bridge. Fifty cents every Tuesday night for the box step and the fox trot, and no necking in the hall. Mrs. Canfield was all skinny legs and startled blue hair and ice-cold fingers when she dragged me to the center of the floor and said No, no, this way, Peter.)

There were two fawns and two does on the road this morning, just over the peak of the hill by Wimpy's farm, and the school bus spooked them and one fawn ran not right with the others but across the road. It stopped ten or so feet from the edge of the road, knowing it had gone the wrong way and afraid to run in front of my stopped bus through the hole in the alders that had swallowed its mother and maybe aunt and cousin. I rolled down the window and said Go on, I won't hurt you; and its eyes were so huge and astonished-looking and beautiful that I laughed out loud. I have never ever seen anything as delicate and perfect in my life. I scribbled notes on it all day and finished with nothing beyond

Ah, he is too beautiful to squeeze gawkily into meter.
He would flash out of it, overleap my meager ear.
Such prettiness should go unrhymed.

Then, later tonight when I visited the still-dry creek bed, I found a fresh pile of bear scat about ten feet from the camper. Big enough fellow, judging from the size of it. Creatures keep a man busy on this hill, but I do not mind. Two days back I found the chewed remnants of beechnuts on my step, and at about 5:30 this a.m. I watched a chipmunk carting food to his den beneath a spruce root close by my window. Something last week climbed atop the shed that houses my generator and knocked over a flower pot.

The woodstove's going, but softly, without vigor or high heat. I like the sound of it as much as the faint warmth. There's ash in it now, but I started it with pine and apple twigs. Annie arrives tomorrow, and I look forward to seeing her. I picked a nosegay of the last wildflowers on the land, including a thistle that in the plucking exacted a misery of retribution. I am punctured gravely, but the bristling blossom outshines the goldenrod, fireweed and aster in the same bouquet. Worth it, even the hazarding of a fortress-sized bumblebee that menaced me from the next thistle to the right.

••••••

Thanks so very, very much for *The Lost Notebooks*. I dove right into it, of course. The book fell open to page 200, and there was a long paragraph on anthropomorphism, the subject I've been fooling with in a unit I'm writing for a language arts series Bob and I have been putting together. (I've also been reading Vicki Hearne's *Adam's Task/Calling Animals by Name*. You sent me her piece, a chapter from the book, that appeared in *The New Yorker* a year or so ago, remember?)

I can't help but wonder, what with how not so long back we dwelt happily enough, jabbering, yellow-eyed aerialists, high in trees and just a while before that lolling, pondering in a nebulous ooze, why it's considered naive, hopelessly romantic, to stamp animals with our sensibilities, to say that dogs can love. Mornings my young colt says hello. His jaws are not built to make into a smile, but I can see the smile in his eyes. How condescending to assume that his nicker is mere, a Pavlovian response to the clatter of a feed scoop. Why, then, is the sound so pretty, so joyful? What makes him nuzzle, lip my sleeve? Why is it that we find such smug satisfaction in arbitrary proofs that no animal has language enough to communicate its feelings to us, when instead we should feel meager about having failed to find a language suitable to them?

It is a thing I would not mind going to my grave being wrong about—that between a horse and me something wordless but profound has flowed. I woke this morning thinking about that, thanks to you. I've seen the bones of dogs, horses, a long-dead woodchuck at the edge of the pasture, and there were the same white, springy ribs I could feel by pressing my hands to my sides. Maybe it is that the rib cage was inevitable—that it all comes down to physics, after all, machinery for coaxing oxygen from our thick air. But it's far pleasanter and reassuring to believe that we are too much the same to be as different as some would have us think. I've forgotten how to run close to the ground, is all—forgotten in the racket and the stink how love and fear and time itself leave scents.

I thought too, what with still another birthday just hours away, how there is nothing left to be brave about except facing decay. Somewhere the last of boy leaked out of me, and I've used up all my allotted denials. Judging from all the literature on the subject, the task before me now is saving what's left. I am already remaindered, so to speak. Well, there are still some things a person can do in the dark of the night or off in the woods where nobody will see him at them and file a report. I can still climb up the silo, I mean, or swing from a branch or take off all my clothes and jump into a pool in the stream. I remember watching my Grandfather Reynolds, a superb swimmer when he was a young man, climb the ladder up to the high board and plunge off. It was a terrible dive, clumsy, crabbed, an old man trying to reclaim a grace in fifteen feet of rushing air. It must have hurt, the way he hit. I pretended I hadn't seen him. What will I now dare in front of my children? A ride on a giddy horse? How things turn without our knowing. A dozen years ago or so I bought a thoroughbred for Dan to show. After a few weeks of training, the animal began to sour and soon became dangerous under saddle. I took over, told Dan not to attempt to ride the horse until I said it was okay. It wasn't an even faintly heroic gesture; I simply figured he'd dump Dan before he dumped me. Now it would work the other way. Where and when, though—in what dark and unreclaimable second—did the shift occur, did body and spirit convene in my absence and agree on these new terms? It is a dismal thing to contemplate. Some would call it wisdom, but it is really only fear. I felt it as an old ape afraid a limb would break.

Anyhow, thanks again and again.

P.S.

Not merely to model good writing practices for younger family members (but yes, this too), let youngsters know when you're going to write to whom, do the writing, and then invite any or all family members to add a postscript of their own. I'd avoid the "Anything you want me to tell Grandma?" approach, inasmuch as it enforces the wrongheaded notion prevalent among kids that older people (in this case, you) are meant to do the family letter writing. Just as important to the process of encouraging family-centered writing, urge correspondents to respond to the postscripts.

WRITING TO MYTHICAL FIGURES

I don't know who invented the Tooth Fairy, but it's a near-certainty that this elusive, nocturnal visitor can in one form or another be traced to antiquity. Odd that Santa, another millenniums-old character, receives all the mail. Perhaps it's because the Tooth Fairy lacks *largesse*. Twenty-five or fifty cents for a tooth isn't going to inspire much correspondence. Another problem is attested to in the cartoon on page 51. How's a person supposed to know where to send a letter to a phantom who spends all her/his time slipping in and out of bedrooms and probably doesn't have any permanent address, unlike Santa, who stays home 364 days a year, same as the Easter Bunny.

(I don't know the Easter Bunny's home address, but Santa may be reached by writing to any of the following branch offices:

> Bethlehem, Conn., 06751.
> Bethlehem, Pa., 18016.
> Christmas, Fla., 32709.
> North Pole, Alaska, 99705.
> Santa Claus, Ind., 47579.
> Noel, Mo., 64854.
> Mistletoe, Ky., 41351.
> Snowflake, Ariz., 85937.
> Rudolph, Ohio, 43452.)

We've been over this before, Billy. Write to Santa
and you know he'll get it. With the Tooth Fairy, it's strictly hit or miss.

Nevertheless, there are those who venture gladly into uncertain waters. Such a one is Katy Vinz, who at age six penned the note on page 52 to the Tooth Fairy. After observing initial niceties, Katy gets down to business, no doubt sensing that an extremely busy mythical figure doesn't have time for a lot of beating about the bush.

I'm in favor of encouraging kids to write to make-believe figures such as Santa or the Tooth Fairy. I can't provide an entirely rational set of reasons why, other than to note the obvious: it gets kids writing. I also like the idea of maintaining a faith in the make-believe; it's important for reasons too abstruse to deal with here. Finally, as you can see from this writer's letter, it's possible to develop early in life a highly positive conviction that writing houses a power, that it gets results. Katy has absolutely no doubts about this (even though she apparently suspects that the Tooth Fairy may be illiterate). I talk elsewhere about giving writing back to its writers. Collected pieces such as this one, offered to a grown-up Kate, make a rich gift that can be re-given down the generations.

MEA CULPA

I have heard it said that apologizing is a lost art. I doubt it ever flourished, though, even in Babylon or Athens, and certainly not in the dim reaches of

Dear tooth fairy,
I Lost a nother front tooth.
Remember ~~me~~ Katy V.
712 warm springs ave.
right your mane
in print

Love KAty V.
P.S. Remeber do not
take my tooth and what
do you do with all the
teeth? can you tell ~~me~~?
wright it right hear ___
if you can.

put the money in the Jar

my own childhood. Never once did either of my parents apologize to me, not even for having my kid brother. "I'm sorry" was something *children* were meant to say, along with "please" and "thank you." Grownups by implication were incapable of incivility or injustice directed at their offspring.

We all absorb such ethics without much question, only to have great difficulty unlearning them later. For good reason I've apologized countless times to my kids, but I've never found it easy; "I'm sorry" still comes out gruff. If you're like me in this respect—loving enough on the inside but stiff on the outside—try putting your regrets on paper, first to yourself in the pages of your journal, mainly as a way of thinking through why you acted as you did (I guarantee you'll feel better for having done so); then in a note to the one you hurt or confused.

This process may sound elaborate or too tritely like Miss Manners, and certainly it's inappropriate to those moments when you've merely acted the way nearly any mortal does on occasion—grumpy, churlish, too quick to say "Because I said so." But we're nearly all capable of deeper cruelties too, the kind that cause lasting damage if left unexplained. When you ache to say "I'm sorry" but can't bring yourself to mouth the words, make yourself write them.

SYMPATHY LETTERS

A few years ago a good friend died after a wasting illness. It was a deep loss, not only to me but to his large family as well as the entire community, a village in which Jim had figured importantly. Like others in the town, I mouthed the common sentiments that mark talk about death: Terrible thing about Jim. Could be he's better off, the way he was suffering. Going to be a hard thing replacing old Jim at Town Board meetings. That sort of thing—symbolic utterances, right-sounding, appropriate, empty. He'd been more to me than a collection of cliches, and I burned to say so.

I wrote a letter to his widow. It expressed my feelings about her husband. It observed that his death wasn't fair, that he was too decent a man to have suffered so cruelly. It listed some incidents which had endeared Jim to me, celebrated his lightning-fast wit, recalled his courage. I nearly didn't send it for fear that it was too personal—that it would make Jim's widow feel even more miserable.

When after two days she had failed to acknowledge the letter, my worry turned to dread: I had done something unforgivable, violated some rural custom about death. That afternoon as I entered the general store, a woman from a nearby hamlet stopped me on the steps and said, "I love what you said about Jim."

I was puzzled. I hadn't *said* anything beyond the usual tritenesses. I looked at her quizzically. "The letter," she said. "The letter you sent to Mary Ann."

"You mean she showed it to you?" I asked, instantly ill at ease.

"Showed it to me! Why, didn't you see it? It's in the *Pennysaver!*"

The *Pennysaver*. The weekly county shopper, circulation 30,000. My letter, my terribly personal letter. She'd done it right—had it printed in oversized boldface type set off with a black border. It ran next to a meat market ad featuring an Easter Bunny poised in mid-hop an inch to the right of my naked sentiments.

There is a lesson here, one that we all know: what is appropriate for one audience can be disastrously inappropriate to another.

And which is why, despite the risks, we should always write to those who are bereaved, rather than send a condolence card, which has no intended audience at all, save for a generalized one. A condolence card is safe; no one would dream of printing its message in the *Pennysaver*. This is because they don't say anything worth repeating, remembering, sharing with others.

Not only should we write; we should urge young people to do the same. It's an old and mistaken taboo to prohibit talk about the death of family members or close family friends in the presence of the young. What are they to do with *their* grief, *their* sentiments? Mourning is a highly stylized affair in any society, but in ours it excludes those under age twelve or thereabouts. We should encourage young people to write out their feelings, not only to those close to the deceased but also in their journals, in a poem—whatever medium they are drawn to.

There are no instructions, no formulas for writing letters of condolence, other than the injunction to be honest, to forget anything you may have learned about the formalities of sympathy. Grief predates custom. It is wild and difficult to bring to words. But we must try anyhow, for one honest line, whether it is from a child or an adult, is infinitely more valuable to another than any purchased sentiment ever written.

LETTERS THAT DON'T GET SENT

The night I learned that my father had died I sat down and wrote him a three-page letter. There had been some things that hadn't got said. That was a dozen years ago. I'm still writing to him. Carried to an obsessive extreme, such a practice would connote madness. Yet I've run into dozens of eminently sane people over the years who, like me, write to parents or children no longer with them. Whatever else death may be, it is rude; it interrupts important conversations.

I have heard it observed often enough that the urge to write to and about those who were closest to us is rooted in guilt—that we're trying to balance the books, establish that we cared far more than it may have seemed. I suppose that's so; as the one species on earth capable of feeling guilt, we do much to honor its presence in us. But I think it comes to more than that, this urge to write to those who won't write back. Also unique to us humans is imagination enough to sense that we can get by this temporary dislocation— that, going as far back as we do, sharing genes and experiences, even looking somewhat alike, there simply can't be any final conclusions; we'll prevail together.

No, I'm not going to recommend your turning this into a self-conscious writing project—that everybody sit down together after supper and compose a note to Granddad. That would be a patently contrived and silly exercise. I am suggesting a couple of other things, however: that the often unshaped and enduring discomfiture over a parent's (or child's or spouse's or close friend's) death may well be seeking form through written words; you may, that is, feel relieved, even happy about what develops on paper when you write an unmailable letter. If indeed there *is* a guilt, you may feel more comfortable putting its specifics in letter form rather than in the pages of your journal.

The same is true of putting pain and longing into words, of course. In this respect, a poem comes to mind. Its author had begun it a couple of years before. It was to her daughter. Over many revisions it had subtly turned in mood until the lines were no longer thick with grief. It is now a good, lean poem rather than an anguished outpouring. The last stanza is almost boisterous, implicitly a proof that revision is indeed just that—a re-seeing over time not only of subject matter but of oneself as well.

Some of our most beautiful, poignant writing is to the dead. Here are two poems, both by close friends, to their late fathers. (Or are they really letters in slight disguise?)

December

Dad, the trees
still are winter gray,
the way you saw yourself
upon the doctor's wall—

ten years gone
and little's changed:
skeletal shadows
sprinkle the roadway.

Yet,
among the spidery webs
a nest of darker life
floats aloft
on fragile fingers, an
offering to the sky.

Frank O'Brien

After You Had Gone

I didn't sleep for six months,
sneaking around the upstairs
of that old house listening
for my mother's breathing.
One night from exhaustion
I drifted off to sleep and
jerked awake to the shape
of a person in my room.
I called out to my brother
who was away at college
and your silhouette stood
quietly by the window where
the pin oak danced to a storm.

I have told this story
so many times I can't
remember if it's true.

Last month I found Uncle Wax's
pocket watch which you had
polished smooth with the motion
of your labor. I pushed the button
to open its face and I didn't
feel the excitement this trick
brought when I was a child.
The truth can sometimes be put
simply. One night in a dream
I conceded you were dead.
Daddy, I can't remember what
I lost when you died inside
my sleep.

Bill Brown

Words As Gifts

A BOOK OF LETTERS

What follows was originally detailed in a *Writer's Digest* article by Karon Phillips, "Books for Your Most Important Audience." It's an excellent example of writing put to the purpose of strengthening family bonds. Phillips writes,

> I once wrote a whole book. It was one of those blank books with the printed, padded covers you buy in the bookstore. I titled it *Letters to My Mother* . . . The letters . . . fit no genre, had no required length and underwent no editorial critique. They were humorous, pensive, sad, honest, always written from my heart. . . . Most of the letters were short, one or two book pages written in my messy longhand, dotted with incomplete sentences and inconsistent punctuation, certainly nothing that would win a literary prize . . . I was almost embarrassed by the book, full of fears and hopes that I didn't dare say out loud. I almost kept it, but my mother had always loved anything I wrote. I decided to give her the letters that were hers. I wrapped the book in pretty paper and gave it to her for Christmas. She cried . . . I asked her not to let anybody else see it. She agreed. Sometimes writing done for only one person is the best kind.

The author found this kind of writing to be so gratifying that she began another book, to her then-unborn child. It's an ongoing project, I gather, that will continue until her son is old enough to read his mother's words for himself. And she has started still another book of letters, this one to her husband.

There is no wrong time to start a book of letters, no deadline, no pressure. Write the book as much for yourself as for someone you love. Record the date of each letter, because you will forget over time just when your child learned to whistle or had her first date . . .

I write my books because I want to say so much that I don't have the nerve or the time to. The words spill out, sometimes faster than I can write them down. The books record insignificant events, major accomplishments, silly discoveries, trivial thoughts. They are *me*. They are my feelings on paper, not diaries to be kept hidden, but letters to be shared.

HOW TO START A TRADITION

Recently an English teacher friend shared with me a story that was impressive not only because of the sentiments it embodied, but also because it offered still another powerful proof that family writing simply can't be over-valued:

One of his students, a young man, told him that a few years back, with Christmas fast approaching, he was unable to settle on a gift for his grandmother. He confessed that he let the matter slide until just a day or so before the holiday, then grew desperate and guilty. Maybe, he rationalized, he'd settle on only a card this time. But when he sat down to address it, he realized that the last-minute nature of the gesture would be hurtful. So instead of scrawling just a hasty greeting, he penned this:

Dear Grandma,

This is to wish you a Merry Christmas. Instead of giving you a typical present this year, I promise instead to write you a letter every week.

According to this student, who had felt somewhat sheepish about the nature of his hastily conceived "gift," his grandmother was so touched that she wept upon reading his card. Furthermore, he kept his promise; every week for an entire year the young man wrote to her, and quite often she wrote back. It was the beginning of a long correspondence, for when next Christmas approached, she let her grandson know that it was the only gift she'd settle for that year too. To this day the correspondence continues.

Somewhere I once wrote that the greatest gift one can bestow on another is a gift of his or her own words. It's hard to imagine anyone not being overjoyed by a Christmas or birthday present like this one. What's more, it can be doubly valuable, for by encouraging youngsters to offer words in the place of some mass-produced, relatively meaningless gift item, you've nudged them toward discovering their inestimable value.

WRITING PARTNERS

For a stretch of at least a couple of weeks, arrange with another family member to become writing partners. This can amount to simply exchanging two or three letters, or it might involve active collaboration on poems, a short story, a one-act play, or, like two youngsters of our acquaintance, first cousins living in different communities, collaborating by mail on a cartoon strip. Partners should switch off after an agreed-upon duration, mainly to engage as many active members as possible in your family's writing circle.

WHEN YOU'RE AWAY

Richard Behm's interest in writing between parents and children is keen enough for him to have written an article about it for *American Way*, the air traveler-oriented magazine published by American Airlines. Here are some of his suggestions from that piece:

- Children love to get messages from their parents. If your child is school age or goes to a daycare center, slip a message in his or her lunch box. The message can be written in a secret code or backwards, [something] as simple as, "I love you. Have a great day." In short, it can be anything to indicate to your child that writing is a way for people to communicate their thoughts and feelings and to show that you value writing. You'll know this activity is worthwhile the day you get to the office, open your briefcase, and find a secret message from your child.
- Before you leave for a trip, jot a special message to your child and slip it under the pillow. Your child will look forward to receiving the message, and you will have established a link with your child to compensate for your being away from home.
- Before you leave on a trip, have your child write down—or dictate—a couple of questions concerning your destination. The child may want to know what the ocean looks like in San Francisco or how big the Statue of Liberty is. Take a minute during your trip to get the answer and jot it down on the other side of the card, sharing the answer when you return.
- Be sure to carry stamps with you on trips so you can pick up postcards and mail short notes home. It only takes a minute, and even if you beat the delivery, the card is a way of sharing your trip with your child.
- Before you leave on a trip, agree to set aside ten minutes when you at your end and your child at the other will sit quietly and think about each other. Write down what you'd say if the two of you were together.

Rich also points out that when you aren't away, it's a good thing to talk to your kids about what you write and read at home and why; and that perhaps once a year you visit their classrooms to share with classmates the kinds of writing and reading you do in connection with your work.

MEMORY BOOKS

A Wisconsin mother of four wrote to tell me about how she had compiled a book of recollections for each child. Every Christmas her children could count on receiving a bound and hand-decorated little volume consisting of their parents' recollections spanning the preceding year and focusing on that particular child. The books included journal entries, samples of the child's own writing, memorabilia in the form of news clippings, school papers, photos, doodles.

A project such as this one needn't be all that complicated or time-consuming. I long ago began a file for each of my kids. Over the years I'd drop into them scribbled recollections, school work I'd find in wastebaskets or otherwise abandoned, short pieces I'd written for other purposes but which seemed appropriate to this child or that. It wouldn't have been much of a chore to pull the scraps together periodically and assemble them into booklets. I didn't, though. Instead, I let the files grow until by now they consume most of a drawer; the raw makings of perhaps half a dozen manageably small memory books have assumed the dimensions of a Russian novel. It just now strikes me as ludicrous that someone who has spent half of his long working career in publishing never had the sense to publish for his own kids.

I'm equally impressed with the obverse. For the fiftieth wedding anniversary celebration of a couple I know well, grandchildren and great-grandchildren (five of the former, fourteen of the latter) were charged with putting together a memory book of a different sort: a gathering into a book memories about the honored couple. I'll quote just one offering:

Dear Grandpa Bowie,

I remember when I was little and you used to take me bullhead fishing in Skinner's Pond how you would drink a whole bowlful of coffee first thing. You used to make half of it milk and blow on it to cool it off, and then I'd go out in the garage and get the oars. You taught me a lot about fishing, more than anybody else. Where did you learn how? When are we going again?
    Love,
    Your (favorite) granddaughter

BEGINNINGS

A close friend designed a lovely card for his oldest daughter's fifteenth birthday. On the cover was a simple pen-and-ink sketch of a lone figure on a desolate shoreline. Inside and spilling over to the back the card read

It was early morning when I took your mother to the hospital to give birth to you. I waited there with her for awhile and then, because it is in me to do things that have no rational basis and puzzle me later, I drove to the beach. No one else was there; it was February, after all, and the morning was especially cold, the sky gray and empty of gulls. I parked and walked through the deep snow to the water's edge. There were heaps of dirty-yellow slab ice and beyond them and extending out perhaps 300 yards a solid mass of the stuff. I walked out on it in my go-to-school shoes. I walked out beyond the curve of beach, beyond where the swimming floats had been moored the summer before, beyond the tip of the breakwater. I walked all the way to buoy 13. I touched it. I wanted to say I'd done it— touched a buoy that far from shore. I stood there for perhaps fifteen minutes. I think I was waiting for some deep thought to come, some stirring, sustaining thing that would be appropriate on such an early morning in February with a child being born to your mother and me, the salty wind stinging my eyes and the water moving just inches under my feet—the world's water, ancient water, not the silly stuff of a pond. Nothing came, though, and I grew desperately cold and fearful that the ceaseless undulations of the ice would cause it to give and me to drown out there, a foolish little man who had thought to hike out to buoy 13 with no one else around. So I trudged back to shore and got in the car and drove to school.

Ed's card idea should pass gently into law, I think. Every parent should be charged with recounting and sharing personal memories about their children's first hours. Not just the commonplace details we're asked to fill in on the lined-off spaces of commercially produced baby books, but sentiments and particulars of the kind this writing captures. What I know of my own first day on earth is only that it snowed. I haven't an inkling about either of my parents' reponse to me. I'd love to discover that my father walked through the swirling storm or that the car nearly didn't make Hospital Hill. But alas, it is too late to ascertain how they felt, what the circumstances were.

My children won't, I've vowed, be left similarly ignorant about this parent's responses to their genesis. Neither should yours. Why not put this book down right now, pick up a pen, and begin jotting *anything*, never mind how inconsequential it seems, that comes to mind in connection with a child's moment of being? Give the exercise fifteen minutes or so. You'll almost certainly discover what those actively engaged in writing learn to take for granted: once written down, a single recollection invariably pulls other recollections to the surface. (I know I've harped on this elsewhere, but it bears repeating.)

Make a gift of your words. Not the rough jumble of impressions you've just jotted, but a mulled-over, expanded, revised version. It needn't be elegant prose, simply honest. Why not a poem? Or a list of fleeting impressions written out on parchment with a calligraphic pen and framed? Be sure to do as much for each of your children. In the event that a child may at present be too young to appreciate fully this gift of words, get impressions down on paper anyway. They'll keep, and you can add to them over the years until the appropriate time arrives.

An interesting variation on this idea came out of a chat with a young mother who occupied a neighboring seat on a plane. She said that without her knowledge her parents had purchased a space in her high school yearbook and had together written a brief reminiscence about their daughter's early years. Another quite touching yet admirably sensible application of recollective writing involves a terminally ill young mother with three children, all under six. When she died, I was told, her husband asked that family members and close friends write out their recollections of her so that he might save them to present to their children at some future time.

GIVING WORDS BACK

Although in many respects a departure from the recollective projects described above, this notion involves essentially the same intent. Over years a mother regularly put notes in her daughter's school lunchbox. They were a mix of trivia, occasional jokes, advice, reminders about this and that, statements of affection, some of them silly, some not. What the mother didn't know was that her daughter had saved nearly every one. Long after the young woman had outgrown lunch boxes (and admonishments about wearing her mittens at recess), she assembled them in a hand-made scrapbook and presented them to her astonished and delighted mother.

WEDDING WORDS

When a couple of years back my brother-in-law set a date for his wedding and asked if I'd be best man, I began fretting about what to do for a gift. Because a person does not want to to be numbered among those who come to weddings bearing elaborately wrapped but eminently forgettable presents, especially if you are a brother-in-law and best man besides. There are three ways around such a dilemma: you can (a) spend so lavishly that your gift stands out from all the other junk; (b) give nothing at all, which will mark you as either someone above all this tacky gift-giving nonsense or a deplorable cheapskate; or (c) offer something uniquely, unarguably suited to the occasion. I chose alternative *c* and wrote a poem.

> *It fits that two should wed*
> *in spring, when noons again*
> *come taller than a church*
> *and branches take a birthing*
> *bend. It's right, our lazy*
> *stream grown loud and swallows*
> *giddying the sky, that two*
> *take rushing April as*
> *the start of them, the brave*
> *glad start of everything.*

A year ago my daughter Laura asked if I'd do "something different" for her wedding invitation. So I did a quick sketch, captioned it, and showed copies to my wife and a close friend. "Yes," the former said, "that *is* very different," in the tone of voice she reserves for unapprovable matters. "I don't know," the latter wrote. "Don't you think it will upset her grandparents?"

Oh-for-two. So I sent a copy to Laura, who called up and said it was exactly what she'd hoped for. "The art's awful," I said. "Just do it," she said. "Maybe you should think about it," I said. "Do it." So I did. (See page 64.)

There's no good reason to wait for a brother-in-law's or daughter's wedding to do something along similar lines. Nor is it reasonable to shrug such notions off with a "Shucks, I'm no poet or cartoonist." I'm not either; I simply try. So should you, at every opportunity. Greeting card sentiments are mass-produced, formulaic, usually trite. Pretty, yes. Uniquely suited to the individual, the moment? It's difficult to imagine. Consider these as fitting occasions for gifts of writing to those close to you:

Anniversaries
Mother's, Father's, Grandparents' Days
Birth/birthdays

ON AUGUST 29, BILL AND LAURA ARE RUSHING INTO MARRIAGE.

Get-well greetings
Sympathy messages

Retirements
Mortgage burnings
House warmings

Awards for scholarship or other notable accomplishments
Graduations

Christmas
Hanukkah

First Communion
Confirmation
Bar Mitzvah, Bas Mitzvah

Farewells
In memory of

Dates of significance only to you and another, along with those countless non-occasions when it is simply right and fitting to bestow words on a family member or close friend.

Firsts, as in

first prom/long gown
first car
first job (or first sale, contract signed, promotion, prepared speech)
first week without tobacco (or candy bars, or bourbon)
first month away at school
first shave
first use of lipstick

JARRING WORDS

This notion owes its origins in part to a *Writer's Digest* article about a gift of words by Barbara Finney entitled "A Magical Jar of Self-Esteem." In it she suggests finding an attractive container (she settled on a Swiss Miss Chocolate can) and filling it with "self-esteem strips" of colored paper, each bearing a typed compliment, a pleasant memory, or a cheerful note meant especially for the intended recipient. Her brightly painted and appropriately labeled "magical jar," which the author gave to a close friend for Christmas, contained 100 such strips. This gives rise to related ideas for gift projects:

- a jigsaw poem. Family members each contribute strips containing a single line of poetry on an agreed-upon theme or subject. A hundred seems a reasonable number. These are then attractively packaged and given as a gift, with the suggestion that the recipient arrange and rearrange the strips into various poems. It would be fascinating too to discover what arrangement he or she most liked.
- the ultimate fortune cookie. Appropriately packaged strips imprinted with gag versions of typical fortune cookie advice/predictions, e.g., "Your dog will be eaten by a gazebo," "Be kind to your shadow," "Don't ever turn your back on a goose," etc.
- likewise, a collection of one-liners, quotes either funny or serious. I'm a

quote collector; I rarely let a good one get by without jotting it down and sticking it in the "Quotes" folder next to my desk. It's a good habit for anyone to get into, and not only because you can gather them up on occasion and turn them into a gift.

- nothing wrong with telling someone once a year a hundred ways you love them.

Finney suggests adding to the jar a potpourri, small packets of herb tea, or candy.

MY SISTER AND I

My Sister and I's hand-lettered cover reads, "a collection of poems and stories." The booklet's author is Lola Booth, an Idaho schoolteacher who created the work as a gift for her sister's fortieth birthday. The contents are wide-ranging, having in common only that they address moments and memories that she and her sister shared as kids. There's a poem about the two of them being punished for playing at the local dump, another on picking huckleberries; a prose piece on a hunting trip, one about an accident their father had. That sort of stuff. Nothing extraordinary, heart-rending, grand. Just the homely incidents of life, the unremarkable details, the commonplace. Which is the raw material of all good writing and which is also why anyone, no matter how apparently uneventful his or her life, can't possibly ever run out of things to write about. *My Sister and I*, like many home-published books I've run across intended for family consumption, is an acknowledgment of writing's obvious and inestimable value in strengthening essential bonds.

It also reveals another of writing's qualities worth commenting on here: it's probably impossible to attempt simple, accurately detailed writing to an audience of one without creating literature nearly anybody will find engaging. Here's an example from *My Sister and I*:

Sage Silver

My sister and I ride Sage's bus
Every day to Halfway from Oxbow.
We wait at a wide dirt turn-out
On Homestead Road.

"Howdy,"
he says below his sweat-marked
White stetson.
We sit behind him,
Staring at his floral embroidered yoke,
Listening to him talk
Hay, Herefords, weather, and horses.

"When's the next game?"
Bette asks Sage.
"Friday night, against North Powder,"
Sage says.

Bette asks Sage about the rodeo.
"It won't be nothin' like the one in '52," he says.
"Ole Black Jack. He gave me quite a ride.
Toughest bronc in Baker County, that one.
He came a spinnin' out of the chute.
I never knew what hit me."
Sage still limped from that.

"There's a dance in town Saturday night," Sage says.
We'd seen him dance, making dirt fly
from the old wooden floor of the hall.
"I got me a nice new gal to dance with.
Met her Thursday night at the Golden Nugget.
Look at the deer," he says
just past the Pine Creek store.
"Watch the road,"
I say
as his bus crosses the yellow line.

"Why don't you girls sing
'Long Black Veil'?" Sage says,
his pointed boot tapping waltz time.
We hum Sage's favorite song as we climb the stairs
and enter Pine Valley High,
Sage's white, flat-fronted alma mater.

QUILTING

All through last winter my wife toiled away on a patchwork quilt. It was for her daughter Julie. As the project proceeded and it became apparent that the quilt would be a smashing piece of work, I began suggesting that we buy Julie an electric blanket and keep the thing for ourselves. She would have no part of that, however; for reasons I didn't then understand, it was terribly important that Julie get her quilt. It wasn't until her mother had completed the work and was ready to wrap it that I learned why: enclosed in the box with the quilt was what looked like a poem but upon inspection proved to be a listing of each of the different fabrics from which Ann had cut patches. Here it is:

Dear Julie,

This quilt was started in the early seventies with the help of your Godmother Edith. I finished it in January 1988.

The one pale yellow and green square in the middle is from a slipcover Gramma made for Grampa in 1947.

The red and blue strawberries are from the curtains we had at Big Moose [a summer cottage] back in 1967.

The red and yellow paisley print is from the nightshirt I made for Grampa in 1957 when I was pregnant with you.

The red nautical print is from the dress I made for you for the trip to Japan in 1961.

The orange and lime paisley print is from the dress I made for your eighth grade graduation.

The bright black and pink and green and white prints are from bathing suits I did for Nick and Jon [her brothers] in 1968.

My summer blouses from 67-70 provided the strawberry, lavender, and chrysanthemum patches; and most of the rest are from jumpers, blouses, and dresses I made for you and Katie [her older sister] from 1964-71.

Etc.

Love,
Mom

Julie would have been delighted to receive any piece of handiwork from her mother, I'm sure. But this was not simply a quilt; it was a stitched-together family history of sorts, its warmth not just a matter of thick batting but of memories spelled out. And although the quilt itself was doubtless more impressive than the accompanying message, there's little doubt that it'll be cherished, too. Ever think of offering a similar gift of words to a grown-up child? For example (and far less taxing than stitching together a quilt), a special album of photos or artwork or early writing with an accompanying narrative keyed to the pictures.

Two nights after writing up Ann's quilt-making, I came across a poem almost eerily appropriate to that subject. I hadn't sought one; I stumbled across it while reviewing a textbook for a publisher. "My Mother Pieced Quilts" is included because it seems compelled by fate, because it's such a moving poem, and also because it offers evidence that written words sustain individual and familial life. It may be as simple as verb choice, the use of the pronoun *you*, the vibrant imagery—whatever the devices, the poet-daughter has kept her mother forever alive in these lines.

My Mother Pieced Quilts

they were just meant as covers
in winters
as weapons
against pounding january winds

but it was just that every morning I awoke to these
october ripened canvases
passed my hand across their cloth faces
and began to wonder how you pieced
all these together
these strips of gentle communion cotton and flannel nightgowns
wedding organdies
dime store velvets

how you shaped patterns square and oblong and round
positioned
balanced
then cemented them
with thread
a steel needle
a thimble

how the thread darted in and out
galloping along the frayed edges, tucking them in
as you did us at night
oh how you stretched and turned and re-arranged
your michigan spring faded curtain pieces
my father's santa fe work shirt
the summer denims, the tweeds of fall

in the evening you set at your canvas
—our cracked linoleum floor the drawing board
me lounging on your arm
and you staking out the plan:

whether to put the lilac purple of easter against the red plaid of
    winter-going-
into-spring
whether to mix a yellow with blue and white and paint the
corpus christi noon when my father held your hand
whether to shape a five-point star from the
somber black silk you wore to grandmother's funeral
you were the river current
carrying the roaring notes
forming them into pictures of a little boy reclining
a swallow flying
you were the caravan master at the reins
driving your threaded needle artillery across the mosaic cloth bridges
delivering yourself in separate testimonies.

oh mother you plunged me sobbing and laughing
into our past
into the river crossing at five
into the spinach fields
into the plainview cotton rows
into the tuberculosis wards
into braids and muslin dresses
sewn hard and taut to withstand the thrashings of twenty-five years

stretched out they lay
armed/ready/shouting/celebrating
knotted with love
the quilts sing on
               Teresa Palomo Acosta

THE FAMILY NEWS

When I first received a copy of *The Family News*, I jotted in my notes for this book, "Heather Cook knows more about the value of writing to bond families than anybody else I've come across." Heather is editor, chief reporter, and typographer of a newsy publication that goes out to households as far away as California and Texas from Heather's home in Lisle, Illinois. That she was eight when I penned this observation is what's so impressive, yet Heather's project was launched when she was even younger.

According to her mother, Jeanne, "Heather decided a couple of years ago that *The Family News* would be a good idea to keep everyone abreast of what we're all doing." The first few issues were limited to the immediate family. Circulation amounted to six copies, which ran two pages. But then, "as other relatives heard about [it], Heather went into a monthly format and included more news."

Heather's mother also wrote, "It's amazing how many letters and phone calls she gets from the family—many of whom write to no one else. The *News* has begun to involve more and more family. Heather's cousins, Kathy, Sue, Vicky, and Kevin have contributed their artistic talents to help with illustrations. Grandma, Judy, and I help Heather with the coloring after the copies have been made. Tom donates the postage stamps because he really likes this idea of keeping the family close. Uncle Frank calls to find out when the next issue is coming out if very much time passes without one. . . . And everyone likes to see their name in print." Jeanne sent along some back issues of *The Family News*. Excerpts begin on page 72.

Heather's Christmas issue was mainly a compilation of favorite holiday customs and rituals as reported by various households among her readership. Good, timely journalism; precisely the kind of writing that, if enough people practiced it, would obviate the need for a book like this. Admit it; there isn't a single good reason why your family shouldn't tackle a project like *The Family News*. And in conjunction with admitting that, why not confess to feeling somewhat sheepish about having been beaten to it by Heather.

THE FAMILY NEWS

EDITOR: HEATHER COOK

June/July 1987

JULIE'S GRADUATION

Julie graduated on June 13 from North Central College. Her degree is in Speech Communications / Theatre. Almost the whole family went to see her. Everybody cheered! The next day, Julie had her party. The whole family came! A disc jockey came! It was great!!!

MIKE, BEST MAN

Bob Andrzejewski got married to a girl named Cindy on June 13. Mike was the Best Man at the wedding! Mike and Bob have been friends ever since high school. A lot of their old buddies came in for the wedding. Gary came in from Michigan. John Luginbill missed it because he and Karen were having a baby that day. They had a boy, Michael Phillip.

BITS O' NEWS

* On June 26 Grandma had a luncheon for her good friends: Mary Ballard, Mary Leitelt and Ann Boyd. They had fun!

* Tommy is on swim team at the Lisle Park District. He likes it!

* Anne is performing with the L.H.S Drill team at the Park, on the 4th of July. She is excited!

* Heather is taking tennis lessons at the Lisle Park District. She really LOVES it!

* Vicky is getting her braces off next week just in time for her Senior pictures. She is happy!!!

* Jerry's mom, Mrs. Murray had heart bypass surgery on June 8th. She is now staying with her daughter Dorothy. She is better.

MATT - NEWS

Matthew has a new bed! He is out of the crib and in a twin bed that has a softy rail. When he gets up from his nap He goes over and knocks on the door and waits for Sue to come and get him! Matt grew 3 inches in 3 months! He loves riding in wagons!

BABY FISH

Heather's Black Molly had 3 babies! They are so cute! She put them in a special net "playpen" to protect them from the big fish in the tank! The big fish are 3 Neons, a Phantom Glass Catfish, 1 black Molly, and 1 regular Catfish.

EXTENDED FAMILY NEWS

Uncle John is taking piano lessons. Aunt Kay's mom died in May. Aunt Kay spent some nice time with her mom in Tulsa before she died.

Aunt Grace sends Grandma letters often. Grandma likes to hear from her.

Aunt Lenore is making a big garden. She sure knows how to grow a beautiful garden!

From The Butch Murrays- Sheryl won a $500 scholarship through the Art Dept. at N.I.U. because her G.P.A. is 3.97. She is among 8% of all students at N.I.U. on the Dean's list. Steve graduated from D.G. North H.S. Next year he will be going to the University of Steubenville (Ohio). Dan graduated from 8th grade. He'll be at D.G. North next year. Scott won a bike.

Grandma and Grandpa's 50th wedding anniversary is coming up on October 23. We can't have a big party because of Grandpa's health, but we have another idea for helping them to celebrate the big day. We know you are special to them, and we want you to be a part of it. Could you write them a note to be included in a book my mom and I are putting together for them? It could be a memory of a time you shared with them, a good old "love letter" or anything you want.

My mom and I plan to put all of your notes in a special basket to be presented to them on their anniversary. (After they open them we have a special book for the letters to go in.) It sure would mean a lot to them to hear from you! Could you please mail your notes to me by October 10? Thank you!

Send to: Fred and Vicky Altendorf
        c/o Heather Cook
             Lisle, IL 60532

                                    Love,

                                    Heather

P.S. This is a secret!

FAMILY RECIPE BOOK

I'd never given much thought to the hoary old cliche, "We are what we eat" until Jessica White of Boise, Idaho, shared with me some pages from her in-progress family cookbook, meant for completion in time to serve as a Christmas gift for family members. The way she'd written up the recipes brought to mind aromas, textures, and tastes from my own childhood, and with them a host of associated recollections. Indeed, we *are* what we eat, for in no two families can such evocations be even remotely similar; not only will our family's chocolate applesauce cake smell and taste differently from yours; the times and places it brings to mind will be different too.

Collecting recipes, you'll note, amounts for Jessica to collecting memories, an approach to cookbook writing families should find particularly appealing.

CHOCOLATE APPLESAUCE CAKE

This is an easy one-bowl cake. You all loved it. Rhonda: without raisins. Josh: without nuts. Beth: without raisins or nuts. So I only made it for Guy. He loved it with or without anything, cooked or not cooked, with or without frosting, in a loaf pan or a bundt pan.

> 2 cups flour
> 1 cup sugar
> 1 tsp. cinnamon
> 1 tsp. cloves
> 3 T chocolate—heaping
> ½ cup salad oil
> 1 T cornstarch
> ¾ tsp. salt
> 1 cup raisins
> 1½ cups applesauce (1 sm. can)

Mix by hand, then pour into a greased and floured 9½"x13" pan. Bake at 325 for 25 minutes.

ICE BOX OATMEAL CRISPS

For some reason which has never been entirely clear, these became our camp cookies. Beth loves them but believes that they can only be eaten with hot chocolate while playing Scrabble by the light of a Coleman lantern.

2 cups shortening
2½ cups brown sugar (1 pkg.)
1½ cup white sugar
4 eggs
2 tsp. vanilla
3 cups flour
2 tsp. soda
2 tsp. salt
6 cups quick oats
1 cup chopped nuts

Cream shortening and sugar, add eggs and vanilla. Beat well, add sifted dry ingredients, oats and nuts. Mix well, form in long rolls, and wrap in wax paper. Chill or leave in fridge for several days. Slice (about ¼ in.) and bake on greased sheet, 350 for 8 minutes.

BOOKMAKING THE SIMPLE WAY

The following instructions are easy enough for a child of eight to carry out. Furthermore, books bound by this method cost almost nothing to produce. Much of the writing that will come out of your family's engagement with this book should be published — gathered, perhaps typed or re-copied, illustrated, and covered in neat, attractive fashion, complete with title and author's name. While creating a booklet's contents may not be easy, the method outlined below will make the externals simple, the outcome attractive. I recommend your producing and stockpiling blank books in advance. Youngsters will fill them up quickly enough. (And, tangent to book binding but pertinent to books and authoring in general, I also recommend that family writers dedicate each publication to someone, just as I did this one to my daughter.)

You'll need fairly sturdy cardboard to form the book's covers. Cut two pieces, each 6″ × 9″. Next, choose an outside covering for the cardboard. Self-stick wallpaper, oilcloth, or light-gauge naugahyde all work well. Whatever you choose, cut a piece 11″ × 14″. Put the design-side down and lay the two pieces of cardboard on it, leaving just a slight amount of room between adjacent edges, as shown. If the covering you've selected is *not* the self-stick type, smear the downside of the cardboard with glue and weight them for awhile, until there's a firm bond between boards and covering.

Next, nip off the corners of the covering and fold over the excess. Glue that to the cardboard — even if it's self-stick — but not until you're satisfied that your folding is as neat and flat as possible. Cut the two cover halves apart with a single-edge razor blade. Make your cut down the narrow margin you left between the two pieces of cardboard. Then line up the two pieces, keeping the covered sides down, so that there's approximately ¼" between the edges you've just cut. Cut a piece of Mystik tape (or similar sturdy tape) 9" long and tape the two pieces together on the inside, maintaining a ¼" space between them. This forms the hinge.

The book's pages will be formed from sheets of 8½" × 11" unruled paper folded along the width. This will give you four sides to a sheet, each 5½" × 8½". In other words, six folded sheets will yield twenty-four pages. Let's say that you have about twenty pages of material. After folding the six pages together, number each page lightly in pencil so that you'll know which page comes next. (You can erase the numbers later.) Then separate the pages so that you can do the actual printing job. I'd suggest leaving the first two pages blank, using the third for the title and author, and the fourth for the copyright notice and /or dedication. The actual text will start on page five.

The next step is binding the pages together. You'll need a sheet of construction paper 9" × 12". Fold it in half across the width. Open the assembled pages so that they lie flat, face up, on top of the construction paper, as shown. Sew the book pages to the construction paper down the fold. You can do this by hand, using heavy-duty thread and a running stitch; or a sewing machine may be used. In either case, double the stitching.

The construction paper is then glued to the inside of the covers. Finally, use another 9" strip of Mystick tape to form the outside spine of your book.

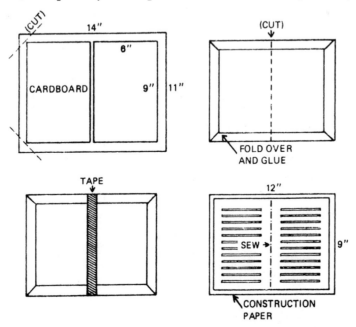

William Stillman's little *Miscellaneous Compositions* bears a gilt-stamped buckram cover; after nearly 130 years, its pages remain eminently readable, thanks to excellence of typography and the superior quality of the paper.

I don't know how many copies William had printed, but I do know that private printing and binding are today quite costly, and that generally the fewer copies printed, the higher the cost. Nevertheless, it may be both sensible and hence affordable to have a select gathering of family writings professionally done up for use as gifts, keepsakes, or simply for posterity.

It would be reckless to generalize about costs, for they vary widely from place to place and also depend on more variables than I can list here. Yet, I'll generalize anyhow: for a hundred copies of a 64-page, softbound book, attractively typeset and printed on decent paper, figure anywhere from a thousand dollars up (less if you cut some corners, specifically by preparing your own pages).

These—the homemade booklet and the professionally turned-out product—are extremes, between which is a variety of perfectly decent alternatives.

CHAPTER FIVE

Stories—of, by, and for the Family

Once, I was sufficiently in love for it to have cost me my appendix. . . .

A story, beginning right before your eyes. A provocative first line, some essence rising from these fourteen words to compel your interest, to stir the familiar but nameless appetite to know the next line and the next. It won't do for me to conclude it in a second sentence, such as "I was so eager to take Alice Jones to the prom that I ignored the pain in my abdomen and had to be rushed from the dance floor to the emergency room." Because that's not a story; it's only a bald, disappointing little explanation. Stories are and always have been vastly more gratifying than mere explainings.

Aside from any direct message they may convey or any specific and immediate emotional responses they may bring forth—joy, sadness, anger—stories excite in both teller and listener(s) a generalized sense of pleasure. It has even been ventured that exposure to a story's *form* can trigger the release of chemicals that stimulate the pleasure centers of the brain—that "Once upon a time" may be the equivalent of gin and vermouth. For whatever the reasons, that stories draw us and hold us is unarguable. Our language, like virtually every language ever spoken or written, is designed for storytelling. Thus, we have always been a story-centered species; it is an inescapable aspect of our being. What follows are some suggestions for family oriented story-centered writing activities. Somewhere up ahead too is the rest of the story about my lost appendix.

TALL TALES

For many including me the most palatable form of lying is the tall tale. Indeed, tall tales and lies don't even belong in the same camp, for while the one is devious, dishonorable, and despicable, the other is a whimsical, folksy kind of misperception raised (but not very high) to an art form. I cannot imagine a tall tale hurting anyone, or a lie that will not. The very first tall tale I encountered was, in fact, told to me by a relative, my grandmother, a woman of unimpeachable character and such patrician demeanor that it remains difficult for me to imagine her dabbling in homely deceptions.

What she told me was an old story—that if you put salt on a bird's tail, the bird can't fly. I was about five, and I believed her, especially because she had just returned from Salt Lake City and had brought back for me a souvenir bag of the stuff. She said this was the only kind of salt that really worked on birds— that if you used plain old table salt you were wasting your time, but that Salt Lake salt had a special ingredient against which birds were helpless. I must have covered forty miles that afternoon chasing birds and never caught a one. When I complained, my grandmother pointed out that any fool knows Salt Lake salt works only under the light of a full moon.

About twenty-five years later I began fibbing to my own children—inventing stories about how things got the way they are, which is the central motif for the tall tale genre. Some of my tales made their way into written form, some— probably the best ones—didn't. (Tall tales should be *told*, not read. But stories are gifts you can give over and over and leave as a legacy to be enjoyed by generations hence only if you or somebody else bothers to write them down.) Most of those stories were downright silly, but my kids clamored for them, often asking for repeats of those that had become favorites. My daughter's was about how Freddy got green hair. My youngest son especially liked the one about how tadpoles can avoid turning into frogs.

You're probably familiar enough with tall tales as a genre to have a few favorites. They'll provide a format to follow in creating your own stories. Don't, however, be afraid to improvise. Kids really *do* love tall tales, the more farfetched the better. I nearly always invented mine as I went along. Like writing, tale telling doesn't necessarily involve knowing in advance how things are going to come out. Begin with a preposterous assertion, e.g., back in my great-great-grandfather's day snakes didn't have forked tongues, and some youngster is going to demand, "Why not?" Stuck for an answer? Don't give one. As parents, teachers, and storytellers learned aeons ago, when you don't know the answer to a child's question, you simply say, "Why do *you* think?"

As it usually worked out, we'd fall into creating a story together, not by intent but because both of us, child and adult, are by nature attuned to the rhythms of stories, know their sounds and silences, their unchanging components, inevitable conclusions. As a scholar of language once observed, "no one is story-deaf." So it is only reasonable that a child participate in yarn-spinning, and most are eager to do so.

If I have digressed from tall tales into the larger domain of storytelling generally, it isn't without purpose. I've become convinced over years that stories hold us together still — families, and beyond them entire societies — much as they did when we crouched naked around a fire, unsure of nearly everything that lay beyond the flickering light. In any story are primal elements to which we're innately responsive; in any story are the origins of literacy itself.

TRANSCRIBING

Inasmuch as we're all storytellers from a very early age, it doesn't make sense to wait until the teller is mature enough to write out his or her tales with legibility and style. When kids tell stories, be sure to get them down, preferably word for word. This can be accomplished with a cassette recorder or rapid-fire note-taking. I like the latter, for it facilitates a back-and-forth typical of good story-telling dynamics — a "Then what happened?" or "You said his name was Charlie, didn't you?" or "I like this story. Tell me more." And consider too that when a young child sees you writing down a tale of his or her own making, a spark of understanding arcs between the two acts; a connection is made between telling and writing, between speech and words on paper. Stories should be written out in finished form and shared, not filed as notes.

Story transcribing can be fascinating, because you get to work directly with the story's author. You'll be nearly as actively involved as the teller, and because you're actually transcribing — attempting to capture every last word, like a court stenographer — you'll have to pay extra-close attention to the workings of your child's imagination. It's a very good idea for now as well as the future to do up some of these stories in booklet form and get the child to provide illustrations.

FAMILY STORIES

A couple of years back at a community picnic an acquaintance told me a story about one of his forebears. I jotted down the gist of it as soon as I got back home, for it was a good story and he had told it well. It went like this:

My great-grandfather's brother was very, very strong. He was famous for his strength. One day way back the family was having a picnic on top of a knoll on the farm, and my great-grandfather bet his brother he couldn't pick up a big millstone and carry it all the way up the knoll. So he struggled and struggled and finally he got it on his back and began to climb. Pretty soon my great-grandfather could see he was going to get there and he'd lose the bet. So he sneaked up behind his brother and grabbed the edge of the stone and dug his heels in. It was a dirty trick to play on your own brother, but my great-grandfather was mighty stingy; he couldn't stand the idea of losing his money.

Well, his brother tried to keep on going, but it was too much even for him. He didn't give right up though; he stood there heaving and grunting and wondering why all of a sudden he was stuck. People who saw it say he actually dug two ruts in the ground with his feet, the way a workhorse will, trying to break free a load. He kept trying till he wore himself out. My great-grandfather sneaked away just about when his brother dropped the millstone. He paid off the bet too, but he was so angry about not making it all the way that after a little bit he picked up the stone again and walked it right to the top.

This, obviously enough, is a *family* story, an accounting of an incident that has passed into lore not only because it is amusing, but because it somehow serves to heighten the sense of familial pride, of *clan.* Apparently we need a body of family lore to maintain this sense from generation to generation. Virtually every family has a trove of stories. In fact, stories dealing with great feats of strength are central to family lore. For example, my Grandfather Reynolds once rowed all the way across Long Island Sound in an old, oak-planked scow just for a lark.

And stories about courage. That same grandfather, an Irish cop, shot it out with three safecrackers in the dark of any empty movie house. And about gentility, sweetness of nature: for Officer Reynolds found one of the criminals dead of a bullet wound and sat for two days by the window and wept and would not ever again have donned his uniform and returned to work had the coroner not established that the fatal slug came from another felon's gun.

And a God-given sixth sense, for didn't the Sergeant's remarkable intuition years later lead him to put the collar on an innocuous-looking vagrant who turned out to be the chief suspect in a murder case so notorious they made a movie about it starring I-forget-who? So I would not dream of trading grandfathers with you, unless it is the other one you're after, except we can't give him away either, inasmuch as his genes account for the striking good looks of all male descendants, and there was nothing he couldn't make or fix with his own two hands, which had a genius all their own. And was it not *his* father who was given an engraved rifle by the very last Emperor of Brazil for some engineering achievement there? No, you simply cannot beat the genes in our family, not even with the genes in yours. It is all there—the storied proofs that we are indeed stronger, braver, tougher, wiser, wittier, more talented, sensitive, better looking than all the rest.

In the introduction to her highly readable book about family folklore, *Black Sheep and Kissing Cousins,* Elizabeth Stone writes,

> Like all cultures, one of the family's first jobs is to persuade its members they're special, more wonderful than the neighboring barbarians. The persuasion consists of stories showing family members demonstrating admirable traits, which it claims are family traits. Attention to the stories' actual truth is never the family's most compelling consideration. Encouraging belief is. The family's survival depends on the shared sensibility of its members.

Stone is unarguably correct. In the act of telling and listening to family stories, we are of one blood, one clan, both a multitude and an entity. Yet family demographics make the rites of persuasion difficult, for families today tend to be diffuse, scattering about the earth and maintaining only tenuous connections with other family branches. We don't gather that often and, except ritualistically—for weddings and funerals—never inclusively. And if we don't gather, we can't tell the old, vital stories about why we are who we are.

Someday I'd like to tell my yet-to-be-conceived grandchildren stories about what a dauntless, funny child their mother was; or how superb a horseman or motorcyclist was their father; or about old Francis Anthony, a distant, 16th-century ancestor and maverick physician who concocted a patent medicine that cured *everything;* or another physician-inventor-relative, Dr. Charles Stillman, who designed a sulky first used by the P.T. Barnum Circus. These tales would be of little interest to you. The appropriate audience is those for whom our line simply must remain imperishable.

Maybe I'll get this opportunity, maybe not. But on the chance that I won't—and because I'm driven by some nameless imperative to do so—I've begun writing down family stories. This isn't a literary endeavor; it's an act of preservation. It will result in an open-ended book, I expect, open-ended because stories are always in the process of forming, and different versions of old ones keep floating to the surface, and finally because nearly any family is collectively a repository for far too many stories to log. This is especially true if we allow under the heading "story," as Stone does, any lore that has significance enough to bear repeating over time. That my father got up early on Sundays, his one full day off, and baked cornbread for our breakfast isn't a "story" in the literary sense of the term, but it's important for his descendants to know, even if I'm not sure why.

How does one gather such stories? A pamphlet (*Family Folklore: Interviewing Guide and Questionnaire*) produced by the Office of American and Folklife Studies advises that we begin by interviewing ourselves. The following questions, its authors point out, are meant to be suggestive. Adapt them to suit your circumstances and interests or go along with them only long enough to establish your own direction.

1. What do you know about your family surname? Its origin? Its meaning? Did it undergo change from the Old Country to the United States? Are there stories about the change?

2. Are there any traditional first names, middle names or nicknames in your family? Is there a naming tradition, such as always giving the firstborn son the name of his paternal grandfather?

3. Can you sort out the traditions in your current family according to the branches of the larger family from which they have come? Does the overall tradition of a specific grandparent seem to be dominant?

4. What stories have come down to you about your parents? Grandparents? More distant ancestors? How have these relatives described their lives to you? What have you learned from them about their childhood, adolescence, schooling, marriage, work, religion, political activity, recreation? Are they anxious or reluctant to discuss the past? Do their memories tend to cluster about certain topics or time periods and avoid others? Are there certain things in your family history that you would like to know, but no one will tell you? Do various relatives tell the same stories in different ways? How do these versions differ?

5. Do you have a notorious or infamous character in your family's past? Do you relish stories about him/her? Do you feel that the infamy of the ancestor may have grown as stories passed down about him/her have been elaborated? Would you like to think your ancestors were pirates even though down deep you know that they were honest, hard-working people?

6. How did your parents, grandparents, and other relatives, come to meet and marry? Are there family stories of lost love, jilted brides, unusual courtships, arranged marriages, elopements, runaway lovers?

7. Have any historical events affected your family? For example, how did your family survive the Depression? Did conflict over some national event such as the Civil War or Vietnam cause a serious break in family relationships?

8. Are there any stories in your family about how a great fortune was lost or almost (but not quite) made? Do you believe them? Are these incidents laughed about or deeply regretted? If a fortune was made, who was responsible and how was it achieved?

9. What expressions are used in your family? Did they come from specific incidents? Are there stories which explain their origin? Is a particular member of the family especially adept at creating expressions?

10. How are holidays celebrated in your family? What holidays are most important—national, religious or family? What innovations has your family made in holiday celebrations? Has your family created entirely new holidays?

11. Does your family hold reunions? How often? When? Where? Who is invited? Who comes? Who are the organizers and hosts? What occurs during the reunion? Are there traditional foods, customs, activities? Are stories and photographs exchanged? Are records (oral, written, visual) kept? By whom?

12. Have any recipes been preserved in your family from past generations? What was their origin? How were they passed down—by word of mouth, by observation, by written recipes? Are they still in use today? When? By whom? Does grandmother's apple pie taste as good now that it's made by her granddaughter?

13. What other people (friends, household help, etc.) have been incorporated into your family? When? Why? Were these people given family titles such as aunt or cousin? Did they participate fully in family activities?

14. Is there a family cemetery or burial plot? Who is buried with whom?

Why? Who makes burial place decisions? If there are grave markers, what type of information is recorded on them?

15. Does your family have any heirlooms, objects of sentimental or monetary value that have been handed down? What are they? Are there stories connected with them? Do you know their origin and line of passage through the generations? If they pass to you, will you continue the tradition, sell the objects, or give them to museums?

16. Does your family have photo albums, scrapbooks, slides, home movies? Who created them? Whose pictures are contained in them? Whose responsibility is their upkeep? When are they displayed? To whom? Are they specially arranged and edited? Does their appearance elicit commentary? What kind? By whom? Is the showing of these images a happy occasion?

Before our most recent family reunion, I asked everyone to bring a story that somehow dealt with the Stillmans and promised that I'd do the same. There was some grumbling and excuse-making in response to my request that the stories be written—not everyone complied—but it seemed appropriate that a family story collection feature more than just one scribe. In the batch was this poem:

Proprieties at Table

My younger uncle said at dinner
Christmas day that that was it for him:
damned if he would ever fall in love
again. Nobody minded him. My mother
lifted up her long-stemmed glass,
some snow slid off the roof.
My father said Thud Larkin said
a horse had run up on his porch
the other night. Aunt Eleanor,
my older uncle's wife, made a little
gravy lake on top of her potatoes.

So just to be polite I said
be damned if I would either, which had
about the same effect as horses

crashing through the door and God
knows taught me not to swear on Christmas
day and even if you see a big red
vulture pecking at your uncle's plate,
you make believe it isn't there.

And someone else had written up an incident my father's father often re-counted but which none of the younger family members had ever heard:

In a dense fog on Long Island Sound, George William Stillman, an excel-lent sailor, responded to halloos of distress far from shore. The figure of a man in a skiff suddenly emerged from the mist. George threw him a line, tied the skiff fast, and hauled the fellow aboard his motorboat. Only then did he recognize that his passenger was none other than the President, Teddy Roosevelt. He and George struck up a quick friendship while the latter navigated back to the Roosevelt estate on Long Island's north shore. Once there, they dined together and then, to further express his thanks, the President gave my grandfather a bottle of whiskey from his private stock, as he put it, "to see you safely back across the Sound."

In honor of the occasion I also rooted through a tattered copy of the family genealogy and compiled a list of names. By no stretch of the imagination are names "stories," yet they are an important part of family lore; they belong in such a book. My quest was in search of particularly odd or pretty names. Here are just a few:

Odd/Funny	Pretty
Weeden	Sarah Hazard
Seviah	Julia Havens
Orsemus Horatio	Matie
Beriah	Maggie May
Zilla	Maria Molten
Lula May	Frederick Avery
Weltha	Ann Hale
Volney	Hazy (my favorite)

I've also been logging words and phrases misunderstood or misused by family members when they were youngsters. For example, I wondered till I was seven or so what a "time bean" was. I had never seen one of these special vegetables in whose honor so much was accomplished (as in "We'll just do this for the time being"). One of my sons believed that "outlaws" were relatives on the other side of the family from "in-laws," and my daughter long thought that confetti was an Italian dish. Is this a legitimate aspect of family lore? Inasmuch as these language-learning errors are unique to our family and help to characterize the people who made them, then yes, indeed they are authentic lore. Such stuff belongs in your book as well as mine.

The Folklife Studies people tell us in their pamphlet how to conduct interviews with family members and friends of the family. They recommend using a tape recorder along with written notes. Today, it's only likely to suggest that a video camcorder be used instead. I'll again quote at length from this highly useful booklet:

> The first outside person that you interview should be someone with whom you feel very comfortable. Interviewing is not easy and you would do well to get your introduction to it in the presence of a friendly face. A parent or sibling might be a good choice. Young children often have great success with grandparents.

> As you continue your interviewing you will pick up clues that will help you find potential narrators: "You should talk to Uncle Joe about that," or "Aunt Jane is a much better storyteller than I am." Whenever possible ask directly for sources: "Can you tell me who might know more about that?" As you become more and more involved with the search you will meet relatives that you never even knew you had! Don't neglect non-relatives, either. Your grandfather's best friend may be able to tell you things about him that no family member would know. Don't overlook other members of the household who were not relatives, such as nursemaids or long-term boarders. Try not to be misled by terms of address. Aunt, uncle, sister, brother and cousin are especially troublesome words since they can indicate respect, affection and brotherhood as easily as blood or marriage relationships. And although they won't be much help as sources of information on family folklore, don't forget family pets since they can frequently be found as characters in family stories.

> Family folklore is a living part of a family and cannot be successfully separated from the everyday activities of that family. This can present problems since it will be impossible for you to be present during every naturally occurring folkloric event. You should make use of such opportunities whenever possible, however. Some common natural contexts are family dinners, picnics, reunions and holidays. These are the times at which famil-

ies would tell stories whether or not you are there with your tape recorder. Under these circumstances you will probably not even have to conduct an interview—just adjust the recorder, relax, and participate as you ordinarily would.

If no spontaneous natural context seems to be available you will have to rely on what is called an induced natural context. The distinction is straightforward. Instead of waiting for a family dinner to occur in the normal course of events, you initiate one. This approach has an added advantage of giving you a degree of control over the situation. For example, you can invite specific relatives who interact well with each other. Try serving foods that you know will bring back memories from the past.

The group interview context, whether natural or induced, has one major characteristic that makes it extremely fruitful. The interaction that occurs as a matter of course serves to spark the memories of the participants. One story leads into another, one interpretation elicits cries of "but that's not really the way it happened at all!" The end result of such an interview will differ greatly from private interviews with the same relatives.

Private interviews can also be either natural or induced. If grandma begins to talk to you about her journey to this country while you are washing the supper dishes, fine—unfortunately, you probably won't be prepared with a tape recorder. If you wish to privately interview a relative, try not to do so under formal circumstances. Suggest some activity that will allow you to maintain a conversation easily but will help keep the session natural and low key—going for a walk, sewing, baking. If you know beforehand that a particular activity is usually a time for storytelling, schedule your interview to coincide with that event. Familiar surroundings and routine activities will also help to distract the informant from the fact that he or she is being interviewed and will lessen the unsettling impact of the tape recorder.

The following brief suggestions should be helpful in most circumstances.

1. Ask evocative questions. Nothing can kill an interview faster than a long series of questions that require only yes or no as answers.

2. Face up to the fact that there will be some information that *you* will not get. You may be the wrong sex or age. A relative may simply not trust you with sensitive data. If you feel you must have the missing material you may be able to solicit the help of another relative or friend as an interviewer.

3. Be aware that role switching may occur. Rather than being a relative you are becoming an interrogator. Both you and your informant may feel

uneasy in these new roles. A low key approach in a natural setting should help relieve some of the discomfort.

4. Show interest. Encourage your informants as much as possible. Interject remarks whenever appropriate. Take an active part in the conversation without dominating it. Learn to be a good listener as well as a good questioner.

5. Know what questions you want to ask, but don't be afraid to let your informant go off on a tangent. He or she might just touch on subjects of interest that you never thought to ask about.

6. Never turn off the tape recorder unless asked to. Not only does it break the conversation, such action suggests that you think some of your informant's material is not worth recording.

7. Use props whenever possible. Documents, letters, photo albums, scrapbooks, home movies and other family heirlooms can all be profitably used to stimulate memories.

8. Be sensitive to the needs of family members. Schedule your sessions at a convenient time. Older people tire easily; cut the interview off at the first sign of fatigue. Don't slight family members who show interest in your project. Interview them, even if you have reason to believe their material will be of minimal value. Each interview should be a pleasant and rewarding experience for all parties involved.

9. If possible, prepare some sort of written report for the family as a tangible result of their participation. Remember to save all of your tapes, notes and any other documentation that you have accumulated (and you will). Label everything with names, dates and places. Ideally, all tapes should be indexed and transcribed. You will be more conscientious about documentation if you place yourself in the position of your great-grandchild who, many decades in the future, will be using your project as a source for his reconstruction.

The last point is for me the most important: ". . . all tapes should be indexed and transcribed." I don't think it necessary to render verbatim transcriptions. I at least am no purist; it's enough to get down on paper a reasonably accurate paraphrased version of the story with generous quotes from the original. To transcribe, use a recorder with a start-stop foot pedal, or enlist a partner to perform these operations while you write or type. If you satisfy yourself with having captured the moment on a cassette and fail to commit it to writing you've diminished the project's potential for these reasons:

- Cassettes are relatively expensive and difficult to copy. Pages aren't. The object—one of them, anyhow—is to provide a *Jones Family Book of Lore* for as many readers as possible.
- It's easier and much more enjoyable to read a neatly printed, edited-down version than to sit through a rambling interview punctuated with *ahh's, you know's* and long pauses.
- While it's simple enough to return to a favorite printed passage, I have trouble locating such junctures on a cassette.
- Cassettes break, wear out, or/and go bad over time. Stories don't, however, nor do the written words that convey them. By all means keep and index cassettes. Offer others, visiting family members and friends, on-premises access to them. *Don't let them out of the house.* These recordings are truly archival. Cared for, preserved by approved methods, backed up with duplicates, your tapes will make it possible for generations of Joneses to *hear* not only a treasury of family stories but possibly more importantly, the voices of those who told them.

What I haven't explained is how to gather your collection of family lore. Unless you follow some sort of plan for arranging material categorically, you'll end up with a mishmash which, for all your good intentions, will probably suffer the same fate as those hundreds of photos you plan to sort and label some rainy afternoon, and which one day your descendants will puzzle over— "Who's this one with the dog on her lap?"—before relegating them to the attic or the trash barrel.

With help from Elizabeth Stone's book, along with insights garnered from my own extensive study of myth, I've derived a system of sorts that makes lore gathering less willy-nilly and is additionally quite gratifying. Like myths, family stories are classifiable by *motif* or thematic type. It has long fascinated scholars and lay people alike that myths are essentially the same the world over—that although their particulars vary, the stories themselves are remarkably similar. There are, for example, hundreds of so-called "deluge stories." They do not all feature a Noah or an ark, yet all describe a drowned world where only a chosen few survive. (And isn't the tale on page 83 about carrying the millstone up the hill a variant of the Sisyphus myth?) Here are family lore motifs I've derived from reading both family literature and scholarly studies of myth. That these disparate texts inform one another is a special source of satisfaction for me. As you read over these headings, pause long enough to let stories familiar to you click into place.

Black sheep
Bravery (physical and/or moral courage)
Coincidence, good/bad luck
Deaths
Drinking, drunkenness (often on the occasion of family gatherings; e.g., Uncle Hayward's driving his Studebaker through the back of the garage after Mary Lou and Donny's reception)
Exceptional intelligence, memory, ingenuity
Family Customs, rituals (e.g., your cousin Leland in Dubuque wears a kilt to work on his birthday)
Head of the family (lore about matriarchs/patriarchs past and present)
How It Used to Be (times were tougher then, but so were we)
Illness, accidents, personal disasters
It's in our blood (we-cannot-help-but-be-the-way-we-are stories; also accounts for exotic strains, typically Indian blood)
Love and courtship
Names, naming ("and that's why everybody called him Steeplehead")
Physical feats (strength, speed, stamina, athletic prowess, military heroism)
Prescience (sixth sense, foreboding)
Pranks/practical jokes/tall stories
Special skills, natural talents (e.g., William Stillman's clockmaking ability)
Success (from porter-to-president stories. Typically work ethic tales celebrating grit, energy, dedication, canniness)
Supernatural (e.g., the night Aunt Mary saw her late husband's ghost)
Superstitions
The vagabond, runaway, pioneer

There are other motifs, many of them. These should, however, accommodate at least 90 percent of the family lore you've just now determined to gather, write up, and distribute.

STORYBOARDING

Storyboard is a familiar term to anyone concerned with laying out a story graphically, whether the "story" is a tv commercial, an illustrated children's book, a step-by-step set of directions, an animated cartoon, a comic strip, or a personal experience. Storyboarding provides a way to perceive an order, an arrangement of elements in a sequence.

Storyboarding and writing are analogous acts of mind. It might even be argued that they are mutually enhancing aspects of the same creative act, *composing,* filling in the blanks. A storyboard begins as a series of empty rectangles, frames to be filled with segments of a story. We're all familiar with the medium; the daily comics are no more than finished versions of roughed-in storyboards. This activity doesn't require much artistic talent, however; stick figures will serve.

I suggest storyboarding here because it's an enjoyable activity, whether family members do it collaboratively or alone. It's an overlooked but comfortable medium for depicting an infinite range of recollections, jokes, stories, even, as someone in the family is bound to discover, for the working out of conflicts and decisions. When for whatever reason we find ourselves confused, angry or otherwise miserable, it often works to storyboard our feelings. It adds an element of coherency. Like fables, storyboard depictions of an episode of bad behavior (or good) can make the point gently but memorably. Youngsters especially enjoy this medium. It isn't unusual for kids to take to it with enough enthusiasm to produce comic book-length tales of 40 to 50 panels, replete with "Arghh's" and "Aieee's."

WRITING WITH PHOTOS

- In our attic are hundreds of photographs. They are old and are pasted in old albums, the black leatherette-covered kind with even blacker, light-absorbing pages. I recognize most of the faces, including my own as a child. I should label them, guess at the approximate times of those un-dated ones, at the locales of the ones whose background details I don't recognize. This would provide guidance enough for younger family members, something on the order of

     Anna Larkin and Grandmother Stillman
     Back yard, 164 East Ave., Norwalk
     Circa 1944-45
     (Dog's name: Buster)

- Pretty dreary going, however, both for caption writer and future browsers. Such write-ups amount to epitaphs, establishing beyond doubt that the subjects in the photo are irretrievably, emphatically, indubitably *dead.*

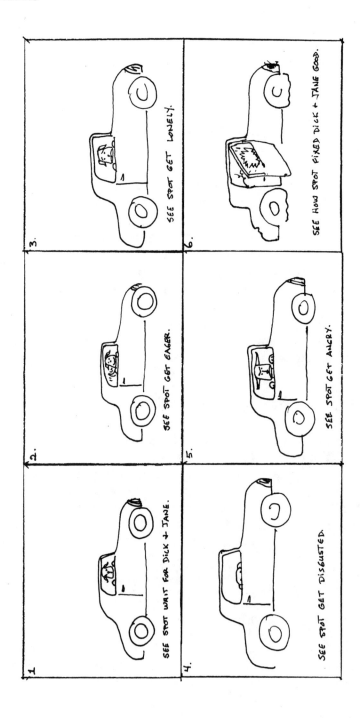

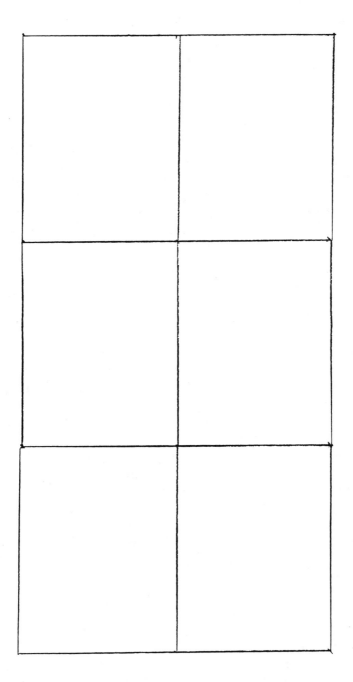

Here is a blank storyboard to copy and blow up on the photocopier. (Storyboard pads are available at many art supply shops.)

On second thought, who would bother paging through such stuff except out of a sense of familial duty? Yet the subjects of these pictures were manifestly alive when they were taken. Why not maintain them in that state? So I've begun, writing up a brief vignette or memory piece in response to whatever a photo may bring to mind. About Anna Larkin, for example, this:

> I remember her sedan — a Plymouth, I think it was — being immaculately clean. Black, shining, memorable because it did not ever look as if it went anywhere that was dusty, or where it rained, or where a bird might drop a white stain on it. I'm not sure who Anna was, other than my grandmother's friend and a housekeeper-companion to a wealthy woman in New Canaan. Anna was nice, friendly, much more so than my grandmother. She liked children. When she drove to the store, she always took me with her. She knew I loved to ride in her beautiful black sedan.

About the photo featuring the three equestrians:

> The fellow with the hooded sweater is my Uncle Vin, your Grandmother Stillman's oldest brother. The woman on the lighter horse is his wife, Mae. I don't know who the other woman is. I lost track of Mae when she and Vin got divorced, but I remember her as being good-humored and pretty and likely to say whatever flew into her head. This photo brings to mind one of her zany observations. When I first saw it as a child of ten or so I asked her if she liked riding horses, and she said no, she didn't, but what with the way the world was going, you never knew when you'd have to, so it was best to learn how.

I've also begun removing family pictures from their funereal setting and mounting them in a more attractive album, one or two to a page and accompanied by the sort of "captions" you've just read. It's a pleasant enough rainy-day task and also a hedge against my forgetting.

• A teacher friend from Maine stole an old wanted poster from the local post office. (It's against the law, Bill told me, for post office personnel to give them away, no matter how out of date they are. It's also against the law to steal them, I pointed out.) He whited out all the particulars relating to the felon described except for the fingerprints and the more or less standard line about the person's being considered dangerous. The rest of the form was left intact. He then ran off copies, mounted on them front and profile "mug shots" of each of his three kids taken a month before, and provided new data: a tongue-in-cheek description of the criminal, including aliases, nature of the crime, previous convictions, last place seen, known habitats, etc. Then he had them framed and gave them to his kids for Christmas, much to their delight.

- While it may be a trifle more difficult to make a facsimile wanted poster than it would be to steal an authentic one, I'd do so anyhow. No law against sketching and jotting down particulars from the collection on display at your post office. As for fingerprints, you can always use your own.
- My cousin Rosemary, a highly skilled genealogist and collector of family memorabilia, decided a few years back that our dour, grim-visaged Yankee forebears were going to waste tucked away in the dark of an album. She settled on a photo of what must be one of the most cheerless clutches of ancestors ever to assemble in front of a lens and put it to amusing use:

Some spirits of Christmases past.
Season's Greetings.

Might be fun to do the same. Nor would it require a group photograph. Certainly your family archives harbor a shot of some lone, gimlet-eyed, frowning ancestor suitable for your purpose.

- Hand out old snapshots of obscure relatives or friends nobody can identify and ask that family members each select one and write a story about the picture. Fifteen to twenty minutes should provide plenty of time. Ask that writers name the subject(s) and describe what's going on in the picture or what led up to it; and also that they let the person speak a line or two. This activity lends itself to readings-aloud.

- For a child's birthday once I made up a larger-than-card-size card, glued a copy of my grandfather's portrait on the front, and inside printed the following thumbnail of a recollection:

> *Your great-grandfather's barn smelled like cut grass*
> *and amber-yellow oil.*
>
> *He liked oil, which is another way of observing that he hated*
> *wear.*
>
> *Every hinge and bearing, every bolt head, joint, bit and blade—his*
> *push mower whispered through its work—*
>
> *all drew on his oil, tink-a-tunk, from the long-nozzled can.*
> *I think he oiled my grandmother, who was as silent as*
>
> *his mower and lasted long past the time when grandmothers wore out*
> *back then.*

BACK WHEN THINGS WERE TOUGHER

In the first chapter I made note of a book by Mildred Dales, *Letters from Grandma.* It was, she told me, begun at her son's urging. She'd been through a long illness and was despondent. But she had also completed a writing course, and her son persuaded her to use what she had learned to capture memories on paper about how life used to be earlier in this century. It was apparently the right medicine. Mrs. Dales not only completed her letters book but went on to edit and contribute to another work, *Five Dozen Fringe Mittens,* published a year after the first book. As she notes in the preface, "Writing and publishing a book has given me a new purpose in life and encouraged me to attempt this second book, about the lives of my ancestors." And farther along she writes, "This book is an attempt to make [an earlier time] and the people who lived then come alive for us and give us a real feeling for our roots."

Roots. A figure of speech, a metaphor for what anchors and nourishes us. All peoples share a passion. It is to know how it is we have come to be and why it is we have endured. Any family is, collectively, a story, a saga told by many voices. It is the one story we seem to have an organic need to know. I don't mean the dry, schematic printing out of a genealogy; I mean what Mrs. Dales means: the coming alive for us of a past in which we are pre-figured.

The following excerpts are from a reminiscence by Adelia Sturm Glover, a relative of Mrs. Dales. It is titled "Homesteading in Montana" and begins, "This is to my children, so they may know something of Life. . . ." Although I don't intend this book to be a reader—a collection of set pieces representing this kind of family writing or that—Adelia Glover belongs in here for what she artlessly conveys both about the handing down of life and about writing itself.

In the fall of the year of 1909, my mother, my two brothers, and I left N.Y. State for the West. Claire and Will had some idea about going into the manufacturing of Silos, but somehow it did not materialize. We spent a year in DesMoines, Iowa, where they thought they would do this. I got a job there working for the S&H Green Stamp Co., but first thing I knew the boys said we were moving to Minneapolis where they had both got a job as Salesman for Nebraska Silo Co., and sold all through Minn. We all liked Minneapolis, and we joined the church there. I got a job working in a Real Estate office in the Plymouth Bldg., while Mother got a job in the hospital there. Everything was going along fine, I thought. I had met some nice young people in the church. I also met a young man from Middletown, and we got to go together real steady, then, suddenly, the men decided that we were going to Montana and take up a homestead.

Well, this just about floored me and I said "I'm not going", but mother said she would not go unless I went, so every nite when I came home from the office, she had packed some of my clothes, and off we went. The Great Northern R.R. was putting out great ads and making special rates for people who were going to take a carload of goods or stock, and that is what we did. Half the car load was household goods, the other was stock the men bought in Minn.

I think it was in February that we landed in Big Sandy. We rented a small house and the men found some place to put the horses. It was still winter, so we stayed there until the roads were passable so they could go out on the prairie 35 miles, and have our homesteads staked out. We had two sections of land all joining.

In case you don't know what a homestead consists of, it's 320 acres. You are required to live there so many months of the year, plow so much each year, get it into grain, fence so much, live there three years, then if you have not starved to death in that time, they give this land to you.

It was almost April before the boys got out there. They set up a tent, took a load of lumber out with four horses, some grub and an old stove to cook on. They would use that lumber up, and come back to town for more. It was pretty cold sleeping out in a tent, but as soon as they got some kind of a shelter up and an outhouse, they moved us out there. If you ever saw a desolate place, that was it. We hauled our water from a nearby "coolie". It was really melted snow in a little valley-like, which was all the water there was. The men rigged up a stone boat affair, put two barrels on it and that's the way the water went. We learned to be economical with water, as well as everything else. So we all lived in one shack until they could get the others built.

I hadn't been there only two weeks, when one Sunday, two young men, cowboys, drove up to the door on horses and they had an extra horse with them, all saddled to ride. They said they had heard there was a young girl out here and they just thought she might like to go for a ride. Well, I had never been on a horse in my life, but I was game and away we went. After that, I never had to have a horse of my own, and I was about the only single girl within a radius of 25 miles, so I had a lot of cowboys coming to see me and taking me for a ride. There was no place to go but to the other ranches and have dinner with another bunch of cowboys. They were lonely and so was I. Sometimes we would ride to a sheep herder's camp and get our own dinner. He always had bacon, ham and a lot of canned goods. Sometimes it was pretty hot, and we would just eat a can of peaches and some crackers.

One day one of the cowboys and I rode into town to a dance. It took most of the day and we danced until early morning, slept a couple of hours, got on the horses and back to the prairie, that was a 35 mile ride one way. I carried the dress I was going to wear in a bag on the back of the horse. It rained so we had to don slickers. It did rain a little the first two years, not much, but a little. I was having too much fun then to worry about it being dry. My brother was taking care of my land when I used to go up to the White House Ranch, which was the owner's summer home. I used to help the cook during Round Up time and branding time. The cook and I were the only females around then. Ha! I was going quite steady then with a young cowboy and we decided to go back to my home at nite. We got lost, but we finally found the ranch fence and followed it to a gate. But I did not get home that nite and instead stayed at the Ranch. It was pretty easy to get lost, as the lights from the shacks looked so far away and then you would dip into a little coolie, and when you got out you had lost the light.

I went with quite a few young cowboys, they all wanted to get married and most of them had a "claim" somewhere. They would take me for a ride to their homestead, but I was having too good a time when I was single to even think of marrying, and I wanted some day to come back East. I always had that in mind. These boys would never leave Montana.

It was 1912 when we first landed on the prairie and it is now 1913. My mother's shack is built and my shack, an 8' x 10' was also built, as well as a root cellar in between the two shacks. Mother and I ate most of our meals together. I had a little two-lid iron stove to cook on, no oven. Mother had a four lid stove with an oven, so we got along pretty good. This was all new stuff for us, since we had always lived in town. The shacks were all built with no foundation, plain boards for siding, then black tar paper to cover, which was held in place by nailing lath to it. The wind blew every day. These shacks had no ceiling, therefore they got pretty cold in winter. Winter got to be 40 and 50 degrees below zero many days, the shack would sway a little in the wind but they never blew over. It hadn't rained much so far but every one thought it would. Maybe next year. My brother, Will, did most of the plowing with unbroken horses. He got the use of them if he could break them to harness and work. He had quite a time with four horses hitched to a plow, and they just wanted to lay down and act up.

I used to get pretty lonesome days, I would go up on a little knoll, sit on a sheep herder's pile of rocks and strain my eyes just to see if I could not see some one on horseback coming my way. No, they most always went another direction. You couldn't sleep nites, the coyotees would howl off in the distance, which is a pretty weird sound. More people were coming into this section all the time, and one morning my mother was sweeping off a little porch she had on her shack and I was playing my piano, when a very nice looking young man came to get the mail. He heard me playing and he asked, "Who is that playing?" My mother said, "It's my daughter", and he said he hadn't heard any music since he came out about a month ago, so my mother invited him in and he said he played the violin and that he had brought it out with him. He was from Iowa, so my mother invited him over for supper Sunday nite and he brought his violin. This young man turned out to be Martin V. Sturm, whom I married within three months. He had just come out to help his cousin build his homestead shack, he was not going to stay in that "God forsaken country," but I managed to convince him to stay. At times I thought he was not going to stay.

I met Martin in April and we borrowed two horses and a buckboard wagon from neighbors, drove to Big Sandy, left the horses there at the livery, took a train to Fort Benton, the county seat, got there at almost closing time, so we just barely got the license in time and were married at 7:30 in the M.E. Parsonage. This was July 3, 1914. The next day was the 4th, it was a blistering hot 103° on the street, and they had big "doings" there but we just went over to the river and soaked our feet in the Missouri. There were a few trees there and that seemed good, too. Then 4th of July nite we went back to Big Sandy, where a dance was in full swing, so we danced most of the nite away, had to sit up in the hotel lobby, there was no room at the inn. We were not long there, all the chairs were full of people. Sunday we drove back to the homestead. Monday my brother had a job fencing a big field for those two men that owned everything, and he said he would give Martin a job and I could go up near the Bear Paw Mountains and cook for five men for about a month, so this is where we spent our honeymoon. The log cabin was about 9 x 10, a two lid stove and bunks. Martin put up a tent and we slept in that. This was up in rattlesnake country, so they plowed a big furlough all around the tent, said it would keep the snakes out. The men took a lunch out to where they were digging post holes and I stayed in the cabin all day. I was pretty scared, since I had seen snakes up there, so I stayed right in the cabin. This was in the foot hills of the Bear Paw Mountains. This cabin used to be a cabin where the stage man used to stop over, maybe nites. I have pictures of this cabin. Later on, our family and a neighbor and family used to drive to this cabin, park horses and wagon and pick servis berries, which grew wild. They were pretty flat tasting but we put lemon with them and one year I canned 40 qts. This was our fruit, this did not grow on the prairie, in fact, nothing did, but we hoped.

Since Martin and I were now married, we had to enlarge my shack. We decided it was too close to my relatives, and we should be in another part of our land. So we moved the shack about three quarters of a mile away. Martin was a good carpenter and said we were going to have a better house. We started out well, built a house with one bedroom, a combination living room and kitchen and a little room aside, like a pantry. We shingled this, and stained the shingles brown and the roof green. I helped put the shingles on and also held up the rafters for him, and it was really windy that day. We had a fairly decent looking house, then later we decided to put a screened-in porch, the mosquitoes were so bad. Well, we didn't seem to have much time to sit out there in summer so we decided to board it up and make a kitchen of it. But it was cold out there in the winter, the water pail froze solid, and we would not throw the water away. I used to bake pancakes with my feet on the stove hearth, and hand the pancakes in to the family through the window. Our house never got any inside ceiling. Things did not seem to be improving as far as rain was concerned but we still had HOPE. Money was scarce. My mother was a born nurse, and had worked in hospitals until it became the law to have a license, that put her out. She was called to deliver about 15 babies out there on the prairie and they were all a success, so the time arrived for me to have my first baby, Marjorie. I had quite a time, in fact. I think I almost died, so Martin went in town horseback to get a doctor. He had a car, and came out, but my mother smelled liquor on him and would not let him in. She told him she had done what was necessary and I was going to be alright. My mother was a real W.C.T.U. woman. My mother said never again would she deliver any of her own children's babies, and she didn't. My mother brought a good supply of drugs when we went out there and people used to come for miles to get help from her. The baby was kept spotless clean and sometimes it would be weeks before I would see anyone. I always listened to what my mother told me to do about the care of the baby, and her information was simple. Lots of things to do that we had right in the house. To-day they don't listen, its foolish, so they call the doctor and pay. It's wonderful. . . . what you can do, if you have a little faith and try.

We had two good work horses and two good mules. They were buckskin, with a brown streak down their back. They were nice to use on a buckboard, if you had one. We did manage to get a second hand one-seater, then we could fly over the prairie. We had dances every two weeks, people just set the furniture out on the prairie and put corn meal on the floor. I sometimes played the piano, Martin was a fiddler, had been playing for dances in Iowa since he was 12 years old. Then we had another fellow from up in the mountains who played the guitar, and once in a while someone would come with a horn. We did have some good times. Once in a while we would take Marjorie along. She played with other kids and then later we packed them off to bed. Sometimes people used their grainery for a dancehall, then we had the house to lay the kids on the bed. It was an allnite affair, because we could not find our way home until daylight. I always hated to hear the "HOME SWEET HOME" waltz. They took up a collection to pay for the music, we sometimes made $5 each for playing all nite. Big Deal.

Martin was a good hunter, so we could get Jack rabbit for food, and then there was the sage hen. We used corn meal a lot, and I made bread and biscuits, no bakery out there. We had company for Sunday dinners, I have had as many as 20 people to feed at one time. We had to do a few things for recreation, so we just went back and forth to each others houses for Sunday dinner. I guess I better devote a few lines to some of the experiences, that I had. We had this nice pair of buckskin mules, one of them had very sensitive ears. Martin always kept them neatly trimmed, and every time they were trimmed, Martin had to put a twitch on his nose and every time he started to bite and jump, the twitch was tightened and that hurt the mule. I was the one who had to operate the twitch. I was in front of the mule in the manger, and shaking like a leaf. This twitch is a long stick with a leather loop on the end, and this loop is put around the mules nose. This did the trick but it was another thing I had never had to do.

Then one day my brother, Will, had a horse that was sick, so he came to my house and asked if I could come up and help him. Well, he was going to give the horse an enema, so he had the horse down on her side, and I had to sit on her head. She had a burlap bag over her head, while he was at the other end. I was pretty scared at this but the horse was very sick and she lived.

Our baby, Robert, was born Dec. 22, 1928 in Great Falls hospital, I had quite a time. Then the Flu was really getting people, they were dying like flies, could hardly get an undertaker to bury them they were so busy. Martin got a slight case of it, so they brought him in the hospital for a few days. Marg had ear trouble, so they kept me there a day longer so the house could be fumigated. I went home, and they soon decided Martin better go home, so he could be with his family. He felt terrible but he did wash diapers every day and sweat. He was sick. Robert had a cold, was born with one. He cried many nites, even the next door neighbors asked what was the matter with him. He just wanted to be tended all nite and rocked, so I decided to let him cry this out and he did get over it. There were a lot of men out of work, so Martin finally got laid off from his job and we just had to go back on the prairie, so in Feb. we took the train for Big Sandy and hired a car to bring us out, went in a cold house for the rest of the winter. None of us caught a cold in this either. We went back to eating corn bread, corn mush fried and all the simple things of life. No potatoes, no butter, canned milk, but we all survived. I am afraid the young folks to-day would not make it. Xmas didn't mean a thing out there, we just all put together, like a turreen dinner and got together. No presents. This was a cold winter, sometimes it would get to 50 degrees below with a lot of snow, so all we would do was stay in and keep the fire going and that was quite a job. Martin did make himself a pair of skis, this was quite a trick, as the wood they were made of had to be put in a boiler of hot water and got to the stage of bending for the tips of the skies, then all the waxing etc. but he did get over the snow a little. He did get a small job at doing carpenter work, about ten miles from us, he took his skies hammer, saw and square and away he went over the snow. He did get odd jobs helping at other ranches, etc. We put in some crop and a garden but it did not rain, so now we had decided we must earn some money and get out of this country. Life was pretty dull with the neighbors all gone, my brother was still there, he lived alone and on sour-doughs. He used to come and see us real often, and he liked my cooking better than his. After Robert was born, we sent away and got a washing machine, worked by hand, that rub-a-dub stuff got my back, this machine cost about $16.00, that was a lot of money out there but it sure helped me a lot. I was very particular about keeping my children clean, altho it might be weeks before I would see any one else but my family.

With all the hardships in Montana, I have many pleasant memories, I still think of them. I have been out there twice since we came East, both times were to see my brother Claire, who was very sick. He finally married a Montana girl after 45 years of being a bachelor. He was a good brother all my life. This is not a very pleasant ending to this life in Montana, which lasted 9 years. A lot of lessons can be learned from that experience, even if we didn't make any money. I learned the value of a dollar. I wore castoffs and made over things for my children. Friends sent me things from the East and I was grateful to get them, to-day people can't do these things. The government owes them more, and they seem to get it, somehow.

I had a saddle horse to get me around while Martin was gone, I put one child behind the saddle and the other in the saddle with me, and away we went. So many things have happened since I came East, I could write a story on that. I am 80 years old plus 7 months so I don't know, from now on.

What I most like about "Homesteading in Montana" beyond the author's stated motive for writing is her utterly unself-conscious way with language. Somehow, the term "style" doesn't fit here, for it implies a manipulation of rhetorical elements to gain a predetermined effect, and certainly that's not the case with Mrs. Glover's writing. Indeed, it isn't writing so much as *telling*. She makes listeners of her children, of us. In so doing, she also brings home a truism: *If you like the telling, you like the teller.*

She keeps the story going. You and I must do the same. It is not even sensibly a matter of choice; it is an ancient obligation. Start with a list. Begin it now. Write freely and without thought about order, consistency, or style at least fifteen to twenty things you'd like future members of your family to know about your life, your times. Now look for patterns, thematic threads. Do some items seem to gather under a certain heading, e.g., Amusement/ Recreation, Childhood, Courtship, Schooling, Work, Language, Music, Media, Place Names? Almost certainly they will.

What's next (although not necessarily; don't let anybody convince you that writing has a tidy step-by-stepness about it) is to pick the gathering that appeals to you most and scribble down whatever stories come to mind. For now, just label them so they won't slip back through the thin veil of recollection.

Now, as Adelia Glover did, simply begin telling one. Focus on a reader—your youngest child, perhaps, or the child that he or she will one day have. Don't attempt to write for the ages—don't attempt to *write* at all. Make no corrections, no cross-outs or erasures. That's for later, after you've let the story pull you along for awhile or, as often happens, disappear under your nose in favor of another recollection you hadn't anticipated. Tell it the way you've told it before, the way you've shaped it over years so it pleases your ear. That's what Mrs. Glover has done, chatting her way through the piece, obviously confident about the value of her recollections, her ability to tell a story.

Begin with beginnings. Here are three that have worked beautifully for the last ten thousand years or so: "It was. . . ." "I remember when. . . ." and "A long time ago. . . ." Don't stop until you're done. You'll be fulfilling an obligation to your family, satisfying a buried urge, and building poise and confidence as a writer. Set your sights on doing a small self-published book, as Mrs. Dales did, or at very least a single reminiscence on the order of "Homesteading in Montana." One thing, Jonah long ago observed, leads to another.

Mrs. Glover's piece, by the way, bears a dateline: "St. Valentines Eve." It gives a would-be writer like me the willies to think she might at age eighty have knocked off the whole thing in one sitting. If you decide to put these excerpts to no other purpose than providing a few moments of reading, go back again to the passage beginning "I used to get pretty lonesome days. . . ." and ending wherever you decide to stop. There are some marvelous lines in there, the stuff of found poems. Somehow she even has her flawed punctuation working for her.

You'll find as you become more involved with writing that it gets increasingly difficult to find a suitable way to end any piece more complicated than a grocery list. I've read this author's closing paragraph a dozen times, and I continue to marvel how she came up with a last paragraph as funny/touching/brilliant as that.

IT WAS A . . .

On a recent visit to Toronto I attended a matinee performance of a play called *In the Lobster Capital of the World.* I thought it a remarkably good job all 'round. I bring it up here, though, because of a particular device playwright Don Hannah wove into the work. The scene, set on the front porch of the family homestead, involved a widowed mother and her two sons, one about thirty, the other, home for an infrequent visit, about ten years older. To the mother's dismay, the sons had maintained a distance bordering on hostility.

She exited and returned with an orange. In the midst of a cold silence she quoted the most derided opening line in English literature, Edward Bulwer-Lytton's "It was a dark and stormy night" and tossed the orange to her older son, who without hesitation invented a second line and then tossed the orange to his brother. You get the idea: the orange would go around and around until a story or poem had taken shape. Later the older son asked his mother where she had learned the game, and she answered that she hadn't, that they had simply begun playing it long ago.

I loved the notion, not only because it worked beautifully in the scene but as much because I love literate family traditions, and here was a good example, perfectly suited to this book. During intermission I scribbled a note about it on the back of the program. Only later, while strolling to the subway station, did I recall that I'd tried something similar many years ago, not with my own kids but with a clutch of fidgety seventh graders—on paper to keep them quiet. I forget the exact line I cooked up to get things started—something about a young boy hearing a mysterious sound outside his window. Each of the ten or so students added a single line in round-robin fashion until a story emerged. It was, I remember, a quest tale, larded with hackneyed ingredients.

But it must have been fun; the next time we met the kids clamored for more of the same.

It would seem needless to list any rules or guidelines for your adapting round-robin storying to your repertoire of family writing activities. Obviously enough the experience lends itself to groups large and small, is suitable for anyone from age four and up, and can be oral or written. (I like the latter because the results can be saved.)

FABLES

The other evening I took down a box of tea from a kitchen cabinet and happened to glance at its back. I've never tried the activity suggested by the tale printed there (it was the Celestial Seasoning Herb Tea ''Emperor's Choice''), but it amounts to an occasion I'd probably have learned to look forward to.

Here's an abbreviated version of the fable:

> One day a gathering of most unhappy people came to a famous wise man. They sought an end to their miseries. Instead of dealing with each person's problems, he told them to write down the worst unhappiness they could think of and to toss them into a common bowl. Next, they were each to draw a trouble from the bowl and take it for their own. Of course, when they read the problem they had drawn, they all begged to have their own trouble back again.

I wonder what would happen if, perhaps once or twice a month, a family sat down together and half in a spirit of play, half in an effort to bring persistent problems to the surface to be shared and discussed, everybody wrote out an unhappiness and put it in a bowl to be drawn by someone else. If I were to write up suggested rules, one of them would be that we each discuss the problem as if it were our own. Assuming the role of the writer could provide the role player as well as others with heightened insight and understanding. (Given a fairly frivolous problem, it could also be played for laughs.)

A Variation. The fable offers a manageable format for budding story writers of all ages. The formula is obvious and simple to replicate: a short-short story (typically no more than a dozen to fifteen lines), usually featuring two characters, most often animals, and depicting a human flaw—greed, chicanery, jealousy, laziness, immodesty, for example—and its dire consequences. Fables are expected to have morals, concise little adages of the kind we also find stuffed in fortune cookies and grandparents.

Here are two well-known fables, offered as models. They are followed by equally well-known morals, on the chance that you may have forgotten how to behave in similar circumstances.

A lion lay sleeping in his den when a small mouse, not realizing its mistake, ran across the lion's nose and woke him. The angry lion caught the mouse under its huge paw and prepared to put an end to it. The mouse pleaded for its life, however, and the lion, who was not a bad sort, decided to spare the tiny creature.

Not long after, the lion became hopelessly entangled in a snare set by hunters. In his anger and fear he let out a roar that shook the forest. The mouse heard it, scurried to where the lion lay helpless, and quickly chewed through the knots that held the lion helpless.

Moral: Kindness is seldom wasted, whether it comes from the meek or the mighty.

Once there was a mother crab who had a small son. One day she said to him, "Son, I do wish you would learn to walk properly. You look so foolish and clumsy scuttling along sideways like that."

"Sure thing, Mom," the young crab replied. "Just show me how to do it and I'll follow right along."

Moral: It is foolish to expect of others what you yourself cannot do.

Now here is a list of morals, followed by a suggested writing activity based on them.

- Persuasion is better than force.
- No matter how miserable you are, there are those whose suffering you would not trade for your own.
- Do unto others as you would have them do unto you.
- Fine feathers don't necessarily make fine birds.
- Birds of a feather flock together.
- Who wants too much loses all.
- False confidence can lead to disaster.
- Slow and steady wins the race.
- The smaller the mind the greater the conceit.
- Never count your chickens before they're hatched.

- And from my great-uncle Ezzard: Sooner or later you're going to get it, probably right in the neck.

- Copy the morals above, along with your own favorites, on separate strips of paper and put them in an envelope or bowl to be drawn, much as the folks in the tea box fable drew one another's problems. Each participant then writes a fable that substantiates his or her moral. This isn't a tough assignment. Fables are easy to concoct, and kids love to do them once they become comfortable with the fable format. They should also be encouraged to illustrate their stories.

- Use just one moral for this activity. This time, though, don't take it from the list above; ask that a family member cook one up. This is more significant than it may seem. Young people are acutely sensitive observers of human foibles, especially since they are so often victims of them. Here, they are being asked to formulate a general truth in the form of a moral from the particulars of their own experience or observations. When an eight-year-old acquaintance came up with, "Lying only seems to pay," he not only provided the grounds for some good fabling; he also hit upon a categorical truth of his own design. That's no small thing.

- Fables are object lessons intended primarily to instruct. Aesop knew, however, that whereas persuasions of the thou-shalt-not type are wonderfully ignorable, moral instruction embedded in stories tends to stick. The implications should be clear enough: by putting in fable form a message about behavior or values tailored to an immediate family circumstance—Tim has been bullying his younger brother, Susan has the makings of a prima donna, Charley's becoming a whiner—you can move past the lecture-punishment-sulk routine to a lesson of a positive sort. Simply design a fable that amuses and instructs at the same time. With just a little practice you'll be able to write a fable in fifteen minutes. Let others, including the wrongdoer, fashion the moral. And keep the experience light.

- Elsewhere I've included basic instructions for making bound books. Certainly *The Jones Family Book of Fables (Ten Fabulous Hits from the Jones Bunch?)* deserves such treatment.

- Fable writing can be tongue-in-cheek, too. A few years back instead of cooking up a Christmas-y Christmas greeting for family members, I did an illustrated fable card that went like this:

> One sunny day a foolish little donkey ran away from home to see the big, wide world. After he had walked about a mile, he said, "It's too

hot in the big, wide world," so he slipped into the shady forest. (He had forgotten his mother's warning: "Stay out of the shady forest.")

Pretty soon the little donkey stepped on a sleeping lion that looked like a heap of dirt with teeth in the front. The lion jumped up, opened his mouth, and almost blew the donkey over with his breath. "You just stomped on the king of this-here forest!" the lion said. "What kind of foolish beast are you?"

The astonished donkey didn't know what to say, so he made the dreadful noise only donkeys are capable of making. The lion got so annoyed at that he practically bit the donkey's face off. Then it occurred to him, "If I eat this thing I got to swallow all that racket, too," so instead he said to the terrified donkey, "I'm sparing you this time. Just remember you're supposed to be grateful." The donkey came flying out of the big forest and back up the road like a racehorse.

Next week hunters caught the king of the forest in a big net. The king roared so loud the whole earth shook. The grateful little donkey knew that it was the same lion that was so kind to him and had spared his foolish life. He thought for a minute about rushing to the lion's aid. But then he thought another thought, which was, "That's the way it goes in the shady forest."

Moral: There's donkeys and there's jackasses.

• Now, for pure pleasure—and a break from all this writing business too—try a read-aloud of the late James Thurber's *Fables for Our Times* (which are probably too droll for anyone under twelve).

BOGUS ANCESTORS

There are few inspired genes in our ancestral pool; heroes, renegades, artists, inventors are in short supply. Instead, our line is weighted with clergymen, shopkeepers, artisans, and farmers. So, both to enrich the family genealogy and to amuse my children, I've invented a few ancestors of a more memorable kind. In the process it occurred to me that here is still another way, albeit a frivolous one, to forge family ties. Here are a couple of examples from my ersatz genealogy:

William Otis Stillman (1811-1874). Fifth of five children born to Tremaine and Hepzibah Stillman, William was a schoolmaster for his entire working career, an undistinguished one save for his memorable commencement address (6/23/55) at Withering Rock Normal School, which began with the oft-quoted observation, "Give me a child when it is around thirty, and maybe I can pound some sense into its head."

Thomas Edgar Stillman (1789-1866). Only son of Righteous and Hermione Stillman, Thomas dropped out of Yale in 1808 and eloped with Nellie Bluke, a New Haven tavernkeeper's daughter. The two ventured to Smackover, Arkansas, where Thomas opened the first bullwhip and black magic academy in that state. In a May 1811 edition of the *Smackover Clarion* a reviewer comments about the school's first recital, ". . . then 'Lash' Stillman himself appeared on stage, and with a single flick of his twelve-foot whip made nearly all of a kitten disappear."

We all fictionalize. It is part of being human and nothing like lying, with which we have it confused. Fictionalizing may open the way to truth. Here, embellishing on a real ancestor, I stumbled on a couple of worthwhile principles. Let me quote from my journal:

> About one of my ancestors, Michael Mulligan, I learned recently that he had been killed when he was knocked from a trestle by a freight train late on the night of December 17, 1879. That small bit of information has given me no peace since, especially inasmuch as the yellowed clipping about the event noted that this was not the first time Michael had run afoul of a train on that very same bridge.
>
> He was an Irishman, after all, and I like to think he was shortcutting home from his favorite pub with a bit of a glow on, his pockets empty as murderers' hearts, and that his last night on earth was filled with wintry stars. Whether these are so is of no consequence; lacking details I feel it only reasonable to invent them, for my own amusement and to make him estimable so that others will find him worthwhile knowing too. It is no different from painting a landscape and adding a blue barn that isn't there in reality but that pleases the painter's eye and allows the next person to come along and fill it with cows. It is not immoral to invent or embellish; it is immoral to lie, and I would not dream of doing that.
>
> I see him in my mind's eye. He is like a crow on a wind, flapping up into a wobbly, unkempt parabola. There are lights on the trestle. On some nights they can be mistaken for stars. Michael is among them, alive still and wonderfully surprised. I leave him there, never to be concluded. My only concern is that he will be taken as a mere object lesson on the perils of crossing trestles, when why I hang him against that long-ago night is so that

his yet-unborn descendants may chance to happen upon him up there.

It is like the grand portrait of Great Uncle Henry that hung in the hall and that as a child I sat on the landing and stared at so often. It wasn't the man himself; it was his tie pin, a silver whippet with a ruby eye. It was poised in midstride, and I made up a hundred stories about what it was chasing. There are just as many possibilities in Michael Mulligan, forever now high over the black water, thanks not only to the 10:07 out of Danbury but also to me.

How it was that I lost a perfectly good appendix was that my girlfriend had determined to skip school and suggested that I do the same, and that we rendezvous at the barn and go riding. Playing hooky was a new adventure for her, but not for me. She'd probably get away with it, but with my reputation as a truant, I'd get nailed. So I decided to go to school, fake illness, and get out on a medical excuse. The school nurse was especially vulnerable to complaints of a sore throat. She'd peered down my unsore larynx a dozen times, always agreeing with my diagnosis and dismissing me from school. This time, though, I figured I'd complain about my intestines instead.

It wasn't that she didn't believe me; it was that my complaint so convinced her that she pushed me down on a cot, dashed out of her office, and came back towing the district doctor. "Does it hurt when I press here?" he asked. "Oh, yesss." "How about here?" "Worse, much worse." "Here?" "Oww-woo!" I said.

"Boy needs an appendectomy," the doctor said to the nurse.

"No I don't!" I said. "It's not that bad, I can feel it going away."

"Call his mother," the doctor said to the nurse. So she did. "Come and get your son," she said. "He needs his appendix out."

I told my mother I had made it up, that I didn't hurt anywhere, least of all down there on the right. She said she never knew what to believe anymore so she was taking me to the family doctor. "I don't hurt anyplace, I was only fooling," I told him. But he called the hospital anyway and arranged for a room. Then he called a surgeon down the block and asked him if he could squeeze in an appendectomy that afternoon. It didn't matter to anybody that having my appendix removed was the last thing I needed — that except for the faint blotch of sin it was a wonderfully healthy organ.

So that is how it all happened — how I had my appendix taken out by a surgeon whose nickname was, so help me, One-Inch Lynch, because I was in love enough to fake a stomach ache. I doubt that my girlfriend would have done as much for me.

CHAPTER SIX

Poetry

I've just now come upon a term new to me: *hypergraphia,* defined in an *Atlantic* article as "a compulsive urge to write diaries and poems." "Aha," I exclaimed to the raven perched on my bust of Joyce Kilmer. "All those lines scribbled on cocktail napkins, backs of envelopes, shirt cuffs, even once, for God's sake, my wife's arm—it wasn't the Muse, it was the crazies!"

Poetry *does* bring out the compulsive in us, no matter what the underlying reasons may be. If you take the medium seriously, you know it to be by far the most demanding. I've seen its rigors beat back many superb writers of prose. But this chapter doesn't attempt to move you and other family members into a tortured, hypergraphic state. What follows is mainly for your amusement—a gathering of occasions for verse. Try them all—and more than once.

POEMS UNDER PRESSURE

Words, even the most drab-seeming of them, are remarkably catalytic. Give a word its head, and there is simply no telling where it will propel us—what kinds of connections it will draw forth, what oddball or beautiful or mystifying writing will result. Although previous activities should have convinced you by now that *words generate more words,* here is another attempted proof, as well as an amusing engagement in writing for you, family members, friends, and anyone else you can shanghai. (The idea, which works best in a party setting, is adapted from a rollicking Canadian institution called the Poetry Sweatshop.)

You'll need a panel of judges—two to three, of any age, preferably with no literary pretensions. That and a clock or stopwatch and a gong, whistle, or cowbell. The activity also requires a stack of index cards on which are printed single words, preferably all the same part of speech (either nouns or verbs).

In the spirit of fair play, whoever compiles the words should avoid truly ob-scure terms, especially if youngsters are involved. (As an alternative to cooking up a list of words and entering them on cards, photocopy dictionary or thesau-rus pages.) Because this is competitive—indeed, it could nearly be called a blood sport—there should, of course, be prizes.

How it works:

Writers are seated around a table. Each has an ample supply of paper and writing utensils.

Each selects a face-down card (or photocopied sheet).

At the sound of the gong (or whistle or cowbell—or even starter's pistol if you have a flair for the dramatic), writers are to flip over card or photo-copy, in the latter case select a word, and write nonstop a poem based on that word.

Contestants have 15 minutes to complete the poem. There are no rules about the nature of the poem itself, other than that it must somehow in-volve the word, should, I'd think, come to at least 10 lines with no maxi-mum limit, and be legible enough to read. The timing device should not be visible to the contestants.

At the end of the 15 minutes, the signal is again sounded. All writing must stop.

The decision of the judges is final and irrevocable. In the event of a tie there will be a 5-minute write-off using new words. Prizes are to be awarded accompanied by appropriate pomp.

It has been suggested that to spice up the contest, music should be played full blast, spectators should be enlisted to root loudly for their favor-ite poet, and the event should be videotaped.

Obviously, this doesn't have to be structured as a contest, since the real point here is to engross yourselves in a kind of writing experience that seldom fails to produce surprising, gratifying results. You can, in other words, play it with-out the frivolity or multiple participants; simply write nonstop against the clock in response to a single word.

I've discovered something, though, about seeming sillinesses on paper: it's virtually impossible to produce useless writing, truly senseless stuff. So I never knock lighthearted, off-the-wall writing games anymore. They usually amount to more than just plain fun, whether or not that's their intent. As for this activity, be sure to give it more than one try; another thing I've discovered is that almost no writing experience works the first time.

Poetry Under Pressure lends itself to community-wide competitions too, with families and/or friends fielding teams. It also lends itself readily to variations, e.g., poems must rhyme or be limericks or haiku, etc. Or you must eat 2 pieces of pizza bare-handed at the same time without leaving a stain of any kind on your poem or your chin.

OSSFERIOUS SLUGS

My kids and I were equally taken with Shel Silverstein's *Don't Bump the Glump* back when they were small. Silverstein has a sharp sense of what's funny that appeals to people of all ages. His brand of whimsy isn't copyrighted, however; I've since discovered it in countless kids besides my own and in myself as well. Almost certainly it lives in your home too. The following activity is designed to bring it out. Before explaining it, let me offer an example of what I'm talking about:

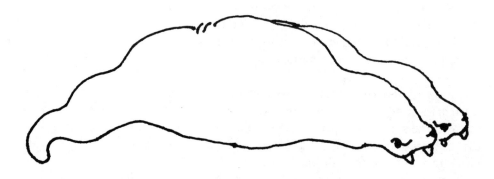

These are ossferious,
perambulous slugs,
who'll slide down your chimney

and hide under rugs.
Count the goldfish each morning.
If you miss one or two,
or the parakeet's gone
without leaving a clue,
do what you want,
but I know what I'd do.
I'd hide in the attic
or move to Peru,
because sooner or later
They'll come looking for you.

It's not hard to rough out a sketch of some preposterous beast; much like writing, you don't have to have a finished product in mind; just give the pen a push and some silly creature or other will emerge. (But if after repeated attempts this doesn't happen, just draw a tree or a house and note in a caption that your beast is hiding behind it.)

I used to cook these up for my kids in odd moments. I'm sorry now that I never bothered to make up little books of them; they'd have made wonderful gifts. It's not too late for you, though. I offer tips on book construction elsewhere, but never mind about that now; binding your beasts can wait. A booklet's only one option anyhow. Here are others:

Rough out an improbable creature, and make enough copies to go around. (Going around can and should include mailing copies to far-flung friends and relatives.) Ask that the picture be captioned and described in verse. If my version above seems too elaborate, settle for less. No reason to require anything more than a couple of lines, rhymed or not. On page 120 is another unlikely denizen of the jungle followed by captions and two-line responses, both delightful, both from youngsters:

Three-Fingered Saddipus

This odd beast is a cross between a
coat-hanger
and a tree sloth.

Dangling Smarticiple

It's easy to see why he
doesn't let go.
He's afraid to stub his only
big toe.

Your turn:

You might also consider answering a set of questions about your creation: Where does it sleep? What does it eat? Where would you be likely to find one? How would you feel if you woke up and discovered that you'd been turned into one overnight? If it were an endangered species, would you worry about its loss or about its possibly surviving and multiplying? Who would you most like to give one to for Christmas?

THE GAME OF DIALOGUE

What I'm about to describe comes from an unlikely source and is, moreover, not so much a "game" as a process of mind spelled out. It is, in fact, a remarkable activity, for whether it is taken seriously or lightly — or "played" by children or adults — the results yield so many fascinating implications that I can't possibly pursue them here.

The late Achille Chavée, a Belgian poet, was sitting in a cafe late one May night in 1938 waiting for friends. He was suffering a months'-long writer's block at the time, a problem so severe that "I had been unable to write one single good line. . . ." To pass the time he asked the proprietor to enter into a "surrealist game called Dialogue" with him. I'll let Chavée describe it:

> . . . one of the players writes down on a piece of paper any question that pops into his head, but keeps it hidden from the other player, who then gives an answer to the question he knows nothing about, in a similarly spontaneous fashion.

> . . . one of the players would, in order to avoid any possibility of cheating, write down, in record time, a series of five questions, and the other partner would answer in the same way. After each series of five questions and answers, we would check their content and immediately begin a new series.

Not as electrifying as Trivial Pursuit or an evening around the Monopoly board from the sound of it. Until you look at what came out of that long-ago session at The Wooden Leg, pair after pair of questions and answers that show an amazing (psychic?) concord. For example (and keep in mind that the players were writing at top speed, leaving no time for conscious thought):

> Q: *What does man seek?*
> A: *His last chance to find love.*
>
> Q: *What is the triumph of the law?*
> A: *The eagle carrying the lamb away.*

Apparently the rules allowed for questions to be phrased as dependent clauses too—those beginning with "If" or "When," at least:

> *Q: If everything got settled my way*
> *A: There would be trouble at the Wooden Leg.*

> *Q: When it is 5:00 A.M. in Singapore*
> *A: Birds sing classical music.*

Chavée's recounting of this experience led me to thinking that Dialogue needn't be confined to two partners—that here was an activity suited to any number of participants, with one person dashing down sets of questions (not necessarily as many as five) and, say, three or four others writing out responses at equal speed. (An intriguing variation could involve playing Dialogue over distance—by mail or modem.)

To what purpose? Dialogue is, for me anyhow, sufficiently fascinating for what it produces to be an end in itself. I'd love to spend an occasional evening at it just to discover what's stewing in people's heads, including my own. Beyond this, however, is what these spontaneous couplets may lead to. (In Chavée's case they led to a 160-line poem, which, if you believe him, wrote itself in forty minutes and freed him from his writer's block.)

Take this one, for example, which turned up in my notes, a remnant from one such "game":

> *Q: What makes the kitchen faucet drip at night?*
> *A: It is the way the world has always been.*

While it's possible to cast a cold eye on these lines—to say that they make no sense together or that the answer is vague enough to fit any question—it's equally possible to let them take you somewhere, to discover a figurative kind of meaning that leads to further writing, further meaning. For example,

> *What makes the kitchen faucet drip at night?*
> *the blinds rattle and click,*
> *that one old song play in my head*
> *to the tune my loud heart makes?*
> *[etc.]*
> *Is it the way the world has always been?*

Or with partners to move sets of questions and answers into various orders so that they make different kinds of meanings: poetic, humorous, nonsensical. Or to re-align questions with other answers (or vice versa), perhaps driving toward a poem or simply for the amusement of forming new meanings. I urge you to try Dialogue, and not just once.

GROUP POETRY (BUT SUITABLE FOR SOLITARY POETS, TOO)

Of all the literary arts, none inspires more vivid stereotypes than poetry. Poets, we've learned, are brooding, shabby, underweight, pallid, long-haired recluses, given to weeping much of the time. Perhaps this fairly describes everyone in your family, in which case you won't need any suggestions about writing poems together. Otherwise, though, the poetry-centered activities that follow should provide some surprises, along with some good poems. Furthermore, they don't require your changing your lifestyles for the worse or staging family cry-ins. I'll rough in basic procedures below; you cook up variations to suit time, place, topic, and participants.

Team Poems (or Rounds). This writing experience may involve as many people as you can interest, let's say three plus you. Make sure that everyone has a sheet or two of scratch paper and that there is a master sheet on which the actual poem will be written. You'll need to determine who begins, how many lines the poem is to be, and exactly how much time each contributing poet has to produce a line. (With four people contributing, 20 lines seems reasonable, even short. I'd suggest imposing a 3-minute rule and using an egg timer to enforce it.) If you take to this activity, you'll eventually want to establish more rules, e.g., that each line be composed of 10 syllables, that they must follow a specific metrical pattern (iambic, for example), even that they must follow a predetermined rhyme scheme. To begin with, however, I suggest your sticking to free verse.

There are no winners or losers resulting from this activity, unless you somehow re-tool it into a contest. It is simply something to do with family members and friends — the sort of literate pastime we'd like to think our kids will someday choose over tv or gin rummy.

A variation is the so-called poetry game, in which two or more poets participate. The first dashes off a line of poetry, either her own or from a well-known work. The next poet's challenge is to begin the second line with the last word of the first. Thus, if the first line were the opening of Robert Frost's "The

Pasture" — "I'm going out to clean the pasture spring" — whoever followed would have to begin the next line with "spring." Not much of a challenge; "spring" readily lends itself to poetry and vice versa. In this instance, too, there's always Frost to fall back on again, using the well-known twenty-eighth line from "Mending Wall": "Spring is the mischief in me, and I wonder . . ." You get it by now: line three must begin with "wonder." The game is played on until a sense of either completed meaning or exhaustion sets in. Here are a couple of starter lines, not that you need me to provide them:

The trees are in their autumn beauty . . . (W. B. Yeats, from "The Wild Swans at Coole")

The winter evening settles down . . . (T. S. Eliot, from "Preludes")

Name Poems. This activity is particularly suited to youngsters (which isn't the same as saying that it's inappropriate for adults). Partly it's the simplicity, and partly it's that young people are fascinated with names — with weaving them into rhymes, songs, taunts. (Purists may be offended by my labeling the results of this endeavor "poetry," but the product at least looks like a poem, and furthermore, I can't think of a better term.)

Players in turn design one-word (or brief phrase) lines, whose initial letter helps to spell another player's name. Let's say there are five people involved, one of whom is named Penny Jones. Through some process of selection (a coin toss? cutting cards?) Penny becomes the first subject. We'll make the person on her right the first "poet," whose responsibility is to come up with the perfect term beginning with p to describe Penny (pusillanimous? pulchritudinous? pert? perky? party animal?).

Whatever it is, it's put on the first line, and the paper is passed to the next poet, who adds an appropriate term beginning with e on the next line. And so on. Penny herself may participate. (In fact she may feel pressed to stick up for herself on paper if the "poem" begins to degenerate into a string of joshingly insulting terms.) When Penny's poem is done, another round begins, building from the next participant's name.

I encourage the use of a dictionary and/or thesaurus. It tends to produce zanier name poems, and furthermore, there's nothing wrong in working in a vocabulary lesson on the sly. (I recall a friend's ten-year-old daughter coming upon the word *soignée* in the course of playing this game. According to her mother, she decided that the word was terribly sophisticated and began using it incessantly, to the eventual despair of everyone in the family.)

Found Poems. Although this activity is suitable for the solitary poet, it tends to work well with groups. It was for years a favorite pastime, and it has lin-gered in a way that's both pleasurable and irksome, for it remains difficult to read any kind of prose without seeking out the poems in it. Here's the way it works, although as with other of these activities, you should treat what follows as being open to variations and alternatives:

Cut up a newspaper into separate pages. Each poet gets a page from a different section, e.g., Fred gets the business section, Mary Lou, sports, Jill, the first page, Harry, the classifieds. Each is to find a poem therein, transcrib-ing it on a separate sheet of paper. Let's make it a bit challenging: poems are to be a minimum of 10 lines; although participants don't have to follow the order in which phrases and sentences appear in the original, they may not alter the arrangement of words within a construction or add random terms from elsewhere in the piece. Furthermore, poets may use only one newspaper page (we used to limit it to just one article); they may not use headlines or subheads, datelines or dates, photo captions or filler items (which for us included the weather report and first-page listing of sections and contents). Finally, participants should cook up an appropriate title on their own.

This activity becomes more amusing/challenging when all participants draw from the same text, which needn't be a page from a newspaper. (This involves a copy machine, of course.) I've used magazines, the Yellow Pages, once even a scholarly journal nobody including me understood. The found poem that follows derives from lines taken verbatim from the diary of a 19th-century upper New York State farmer. Read as such, it was dull going. Yet look what I discovered in these crabbed, two- to three-line entries spanning the years 1838-1840:

Shower at Even

James Steel went past
with the sleigh and the bells,
the wind ahowling on the house
all smokey like Indian summer.

the sap run fast, the rime
was white, the anchor ice remained.
John carried my Coat to Eri Gray's
and old Sam Kinion come.

the Bees was out like summer,

another ewe had twins.
we threshed with the horses
and some with the Flails and I
drawed some stone and dung.

we mowed in the head of the meddow
and the wind blows up
like a storm. the dampness is
aflying and it looks
some like a storm.

This one was derived from a brief article in the Tuesday science section of the *New York Times.*

Outside Aptos

Outside Aptos in Santa Cruz County a frog
may have as many legs as eight.
It's all right. Quite and unex-
traneous and, outside Aptos anyway,
not the kind of thing we fuss about.

These found poems both come from the same article, again from the *Times.* Both were "written" within minutes of one another. In neither case has a single word been changed or added.

I kissed her goodbye
thinking this was the last
time I'd touch her face.

A tiny street, feathers
floating in the air,
gestured heavenward.

Thank God I lived
for the day. Farewell
forever, my daughter.
There is no need to worry.

· · · · · ·

There will always be
rabbis in Samarkand.
Through the reigns of
Ghengis Khan and Tamerlane,
riding donkeys or drinking
green tea—all of them
natives. There is no
need to worry. The teachings
go on.

And this one came from the *Harbrace College Handbook* correction chart, a delightfully ironic source, given the poem's subject matter and the stuffy nature of the handbook.

HE, SHE, IT: A Freshman Composition Teacher on the Arts of Love

Vague reference, ambiguous, supplying enough information:
Dangling modifier, brackets.

Transitional expressions, distinctions between shall and will,
Plural form, singular meaning.
Tense mood.
Completion of comparisons, etc.
Agreement: Nonrestrictive elements.

Proper materials, appropriate tense forms, length, beginning.
Conjunction:
Linking by parallel structure,
Linking by repetition:
Unity and coherence.

Short, choppy sentences, special words.
Confusion of EI and IE,
AND WHO, AND WHICH, I and O.
Each, either, etc.,
Other fragments.
Coordination and subordination, indicating possession.

Over use for emphasis.
Avoiding excessive length.
Good use, variety, combination of methods.
Cause and effect:

Climax.
Unusual order.
Beginnings and endings.

Charles David Wright and Ruth Wright

Although the term *found poems* suggests that it's up to you to seek out your own sources, I've provided some prose as a possible source of your first subject. It's a page from a fusty, two-volume encyclopedia of sport, published in London in 1897. There are at least a dozen poems here. As in all cases involving found poems, what you end up with must have nothing at all to do with the subject (here, the sport of curling) of the piece you draw from.

Curling is the most characteristic of Scottish sports, and in one form or other has been practised in that country for more than four centuries back. From some of the words found in the glossary annexed hereto, — such as Kuting, Rink, Bonspiel, Tee, etc., — some have maintained that the game was introduced into Scotland from the Low Countries, but this inference from etymology is contradicted by historical facts, and there is little doubt that curling, in its origin as in its development, is peculiarly Scottish. Although now to be found in most other countries where ice abounds, there is always a Scottish ring about the game, and even more than golf, which has now spread over the world, it is regarded as a national sport, the title generally given to it by its devotees being—"Scotland's ain game." At first the game seems to have been a kind of quoiting on the ice, a stone rounded by some river and weighing a few pounds being used, with a niche for the thumb on one side, and one for the fingers on the other. With a curving sweep from behind, the player pitched his large pebble, and the ice carried it to the tee or mark aimed at, the thrower making due allowance for the nature of the surface in delivering his shot. This was the Kuting-Stone or Pilty-cock period of curling. Next came the Giant, or Boulder age, when the curler took a large boulder or block from the river-bed, inserted a rough iron handle therein, and propelled it along the ice to the desired goal. The variety of weight and shape of stone during this period must have been infinite, for while 60 lbs. was about the minimum, we hear of some stones which actually weighed 200 lbs., and one is on exhibition which turns the scale at 117 lbs. Each player used one stone, and when the many-shaped boulders lay around the Gogsee or Tozee they must have had a motley appearance, and some of their owners must have been giants. About the middle of last century the curling stone was found in a more civilised shape, the formation of clubs for the purpose of enjoying the sport having a good deal to do with the improvement. By the end of the century the stones were all rounded with more or less precision, though some were still rather uncouth in appearance, and the variety of chiselling so great, that force rather than scientific accuracy ruled the play. The two most renowned curling clubs of last century were the Canonmills and the Duddingston clubs. As a proof of the national character of the game, it may be stated that in the Scottish capital the magistrates used to march in procession, headed by a band playing the *Curler's March,* to open the winter's sport on the Nor' Loch, where the Edinburgh curlers played before they were driven therefrom to Canonmills when the Loch was drained dry for city improvements. In the history of this popular pastime, the most important event was the institution in 1838 of the Grand Caledonian Curling Club, the object of which was to be a Curling Union, in which all clubs would be associated, and which, by representatives from all its clubs annually convened as a curling parliament, would regulate the laws of the game at home and abroad. This association or union has been most successful, and it may safely be said that no sport is so admirably supervised and regulated as Curling, a fact which is due to the admirable way in which the business of the head club is conducted.

Curling, like golf, is not only ancient, but also royal. There are some shadowy traditions that several of the Stuart kings played the game: and the unfortunate Darnley, who was for a time husband of the still more unfortunate Queen Mary, is reputed to have been a curler. When the Prince Consort and her Majesty the Queen were on visit to Scotland, they were initiated into the mysteries of the game by the Earl of Mansfield, then President of the Grand Club, and the Prince then agreed to become its patron. Soon after, the club received permission to wear the title ''Royal,'' and as ''The Royal Caledonian Curling Club'' it has continued to preside over the sport. From its institution may be dated the great improvement that has made the game one of the most scientific, and required the development of the stones on such lines that they are now ''things of beauty.''

Another variation is to turn poets loose with a pad and pencil in a hardware store or supermarket or antique shop—anyplace featuring a wide and perhaps bewildering variety of merchandise. The idea is to list items and then subsequently to combine them in ways that make for poetry—that please the maker's eye and ear. Here's an example. Whether or not it's poetry I'll leave up to you to determine:

> *On the shelves*
> *of our general store*
> *you can find*
> *eyebolts, stovebolts, U-bolts and carriage bolts;*
> *birdfood, catfood, dogfood, and fishfood;*
> *birthday cards, Christmas cards, Easter and condolence*
> *   cards;*
> *rubbers, galoshes, barn boots and Gorilla-brand workshoes;*
> *kite string, ribbon, rope, and chain.*
> *Oh, and*
> *notebooks, envelopes, liver pills and handkerchiefs;*
> *Copenhagen, O.B. Joyful, Redman, and plug;*
> *shotgun shells, deer slugs, .22's and thirty-ought-sixes;*
> *inner tubes, long underwear, hair spray and dental floss;*
> *wallets, purses, Big Ben clocks and pantyhose;*
> *jackknives, boning knives, steak knives, and skinning knives;*
> *And the next aisle over*
> *fishhooks, lures, lines, and nets;*
> *rocksalt, potting soil, pie tins and Aspergum;*
> *coveralls, sparkplugs, pump leathers and teething rings;*
> *Jujubes, licorice whips, gumdrops and Tootsie Rolls;*
> *heating pads, hot water bottles, Posted signs and valve cores;*
> *beads, brooches, bracelets, and 3 kinds of suspenders;*
> *pocketcombs, pencils, pens and erasers;*
> *brush saws, pliers, drill bits and hammers;*
> *smoke pipe, septic pipe, copper pipe and pipe cleaners;*
> *fennel, dill, anise, and cinnamon;*
> *flux, solder, welding rod and rivets. . . .*
> *I'm just skimming.*

Still another variation on the found poem occurred to Rosemary Deen, a friend and poet, who asserted once that it's perfectly simple to find poems hiding in dictionary definitions and shortly thereafter sent a convincing sample, which I've since misplaced. I just now flipped my *Webster's Ninth New Collegiate* open, however. Let's see what I come up with, using only one definition per term and sticking to just one page. I'll give myself five minutes.

Inner Light

Incapable of being wounded,
inaccessible to view,
call forth by incantation
a maiden loved by Zeus.

Something going here; not sure what but something caught between *investiture* and *iodizing* that the editors didn't have in mind. Another five minutes (or five years) and I'd have uncovered it. What has always impressed me about found poems is that it is apparently a near-impossibility to avoid generating meaning. It seems as irresistible as spelling out words in alphabet soup that we tease out our own order, rationality from chanced-upon phrases. Finding poems, beneath its apparent inconsequence, involves deep uses of the imagination. It's also fun.

Concrete Poems. Although a poem can never *be* the thing it describes or considers, the concrete (or spatial) poem uses arrangements of letters and words to give typographic shape to the poem's meaning. Concrete poems lend themselves to group or partnered authoring in ways that should be obvious, but they're probably even more engaging as a solitary pastime, or, ideally, for friends and family members to work at individually, then share. Some examples are on page 132.

Scatter Poems. Scatter poems needn't be group efforts either. That's the way we've always proceeded with them, however—and besides, this *is* a book mainly about family writing activities, not poetry writing *per se*. What's a scatter poem? Something between a found poem and a ransom note, I suppose. To make them requires your gathering various word sources featuring a variety of typographical styles and sizes—brochures, junk mail, magazines, last year's Yellow Pages, backs of cereal boxes . . . any two-dimensional word-bearing materials that will yield to scissors or X-acto knife.

Then, simply clip and glue, allowing the poem to discover its meaning along the way; or, if you're the methodical sort, laying the whole thing out in advance. Some examples are on pages 133 and 134.

```
                    O,O
                     n
                     t
                     h
                     e
                     o
                    ther
                  hand, th
                 ere is somet
               hing to be said f
              or—I mean I've come
              around to appreci
                 ating the vir
                   tues of-
                    - ce
                     l
                     i
                     b
                     a
                    c y


                   ......
         What do you see when you trot?

    Not        aw       lot.
         an        ful

                   ......
                    R
                     A
                     I
                     N
                      '

                       '

                       '

                        '

                        '


                        .
                        :
                        :
                 r          n
                   a . i
```

CURIOUS

Heart

BEWARE

the

ONE DARK SEASON ,

Reason

We FISH

FOR

TIME time TIME

listen

QUICK Spirit

remember

My rules for scatter poems are that only single words may be used—no sentences or phrases; and that poems be appropriately titled, punctuated, and capitalized. My other rule is that they make sense, although this is an unenforceable dictum which nearly everyone ignored. Better to make up your own rules or proceed without any.

You'll probably find, as we did, that the shapes, colors, and textures of the words will begin to influence you nearly as much as their literal meanings—that there is an additional and compelling aesthetic dimension to this kind of poetry. For that matter, scatter poems are classifiably a graphic arts medium. I've seen striking examples of poster-size works hung from walls, and scaled-down scatter poems used as greeting cards.

Perhaps you have already determined that this activity is ideal for very young children. Indeed it is. Even those too young to form letters or wield scissors love to arrange bright-colored words into "poems" or "stories," whose meanings they're eager to share. One couple I know keeps hundreds of clipped-out words (most of them glued to sturdy stock) in a large paper bag. On rainy days their preschooler dumps them on the floor and amuses herself composing poem after poem, each of which she "reads" to her parents. Aside from its amusement value, such an activity immeasurably enriches a child's early grounding in literacy. (I confess to being dubious, though, about the claim that three-and-a-half-year-old Sarah writes better stuff than most adult poets.)

The Cinquain. This is a simple poetic form, simpler even than that of haiku. It's also nearly perfect for round-robin poetry writing. The cinquain is a five-line poem in which the first line has one word, the second line, two words, the third line, three words, the fourth line, four words, and the fifth line, one. (A variation: two, four, six, eight, and two lines.) To make a group cinquain, the first person simply puts down any word that comes to mind and passes the paper to the next poet, who makes the second line by writing two words. Etc. As will soon become obvious, the person responsible for line five, the one-word conclusion, has the devilish job of pulling the entire poem together. Thus, I'd suggest rotating the order of poets, especially if you sense that poet number four secretly hates poet number five.

Although I've labeled the cinquain a simple form, it's far more than a vehicle for light verse or pure nonsense. Perhaps because there are no metrical or syllabic limitations, cinquains seem to house a power far beyond their eleven-word dimensions (but don't take them all that seriously; you can also produce perfectly goofy cinquains without guilt).

Here are examples. One was produced by a group of three adults, one by three adolescents, ages 12 to 14; and two by an individual. You figure out which is which.

> *Two*
> *Pale moons*
> *Light longer than*
> *Weavers' fingers or two*
> *Moths.*

> *Blue*
> *Is cold*
> *Blood running under*
> *And over the same*
> *Stones.*

> Why
> *Is not*
> *I agree nearly as*
> *Terrifying a matter as*
> When.

> *If*
> *You wiped*
> *The ketchup off*
> *Your tie, I might*
> *Agree.*

Haiku. The traditional three-line Japanese haiku form is inflexible. The first line has five syllables, the second, seven syllables, and the third, five syllables. There's more to it than this, however; you could easily concoct a grocery list broken into the same line and syllable counts—

> *grape juice, tuna, bread,*
> *mozzarella, garlic salt,*
> *pig's feet, chewing gum*

but it's clearly not in the spirit of poetry. Indeed, I do not remember ever having seen a less appealing dungheap of words. Like much else that we associate with Japanese aesthetics, the haiku is spare, delicate, and highly focused—a seventeen-syllable miniature, usually of some image from nature.

I find the form quite difficult, probably because it is so exacting. As a teacher and parent, however, I've noted that young people (although not too young; perhaps ten and up) are able to produce lovely haiku seemingly without effort. Look at these examples, which were produced by youngsters:

Water insects hem
The pool, each lifting lightly
As morning vapor.

For every kiss
A city falls to ruins.
Therefore cling to me.

The purple of a
Swallow's breast is the purple
Of a summer storm.

Try one. Every day for a week. And please do this too: each morning of the week, pin the new haiku up on the writers' bulletin board. What better way to say Good morning?

The Limerick. This is a limerick:

There was a young man from Dundee
Who was driven quite mad by a flea.
When he screamed, "I must scratch it!"
His wife gave him a hatchet,
Which impressed the young man from Dundee.

Limericks are mostly funny, some more so than others. Nearly everybody likes to make them up, including children, most of whom know the rhyme scheme and meter of limericks before they're nine. There isn't much to say about the limerick, then, except to point out the obvious: that they're five lines long, have an obvious meter: da-DA-DA-da-DA-DA-da-DA, and an emphatic rhyme scheme: lines 1, 2, and 5 must rhyme, and so must lines 3 and 4. Instead of going on about them, let me offer a few more models, enough to sharpen your ear. Round-robin limericks? Sure, why not? Or write/borrow the first four lines and ask someone else to provide the clincher.

> *There was an old man from Nantucket*
> *Who kept all his cash in a bucket.*
> *But his daughter, named Nan,*
> *Ran away with a man,*
> *And as for the bucket, Nantucket.*

> *There was a young laddie named Hall,*
> *Who fell in a spring in the fall.*
> *'Twould have been a sad thing*
> *If he'd died in the spring,*
> *But as noted he died in the fall.*

> *Said a miser while counting his money,*
> *"Two cents missing—now isn't that funny."*
> *So he laughed about that*
> *While kicking the cat,*
> *(You provide the last line.)*

Couplets. Couplets, unlike sonnets or sestinas or villanelles, are very simple. Even preschoolers, who delight in rhyme even if they can't yet write it, are capable of creating couplets (which should be transcribed and entered in the child's writing folder, along with the picture you've asked them to draw of each poem).

There are no rules for couplets, other than that they are two lines long and rhyme, as in

> My cat is white.   Bees make honey.
> She doesn't bite.   I think that's funny.

In his excellent book, *Any Child Can Write,* Harvey Weiner suggests that parents leave out the last word of the second line, to see what youngsters come up with. I'd also try giving them a first line and asking that they provide the second one. It's a promising notion too to string some of your child's couplets together—with his or her help, of course—into a larger poem, perhaps eight or ten lines about animals or friends or utter nonsense.

Septones. This idea comes from a publication put out by the California Teachers of English, *Idea Seeds.* It's as nicely suited to at-home poetry sessions, however, as it is to the classroom, no matter what the ages of participants. A septone is a poem in which the number of syllables per line corresponds to the numbers in the poet's telephone number. Thus, 435-6423 could produce something like the following:

> *I like to think (4 syllables)*
> *that I will (3)*
> *always know the way, (5)*
> *no matter how dark the (6)*
> *stairs, the long hall, (4)*
> *back to (2)*
> *yesterday. (3)*

Obviously enough, you can expand the form to ten lines by including the area code or reduce it to five lines by using your zip code rather than phone number. Such an activity might work well on long auto trips, based on license plate numbers. Youngsters may also be drawn to the idea because it can function as a secret code of sorts. (For kids too young to be familiar with syllabication, whole words may be substituted for syllables.)

Riddle Poems.

> *I think that I shall never see*
> *A vegetable that's oranger than me.*

> *I am a color made of blue and yellow,*
> *the same as that giant, jolly fellow.*

You get the idea (but even if you don't, I'm not going to sit here cooking up still more silly riddles until you do).

Definition Poems. In some respects, the simplest of all. Definition poems work very well in group settings too. It's easy to see why. Someone—why not you?—provides a word, let's say "Loneliness." Others add a line each, fleshing out the definition in subjective, personalized terms:

> *Loneliness*
> *Is an empty mailbox,*
> *Waking,*
> *Peanut shells littering the livingroom floor,*
> *A trumpet in the rain,*
> *The neighbor's phone ringing,*
> *Etc. (Why not finish it yourself?)*

I've seen a definition poem run on to over a hundred lines, maintaining a group in rapt concentration. This is an experience to try more than once, whether the subject is heavy or light.

Starters. To get the poets in your family cranking out verse, here are some reliably provocative lines, the first two thanks to the late William Carlos Williams.

> *This is just to say*
>
> *So much depends upon*
>
> *If I had my way*
>
> *I like the sound [smell, taste, touch, sight] of*
>
> *I love the way*
>
> *If I hold it up to the light*
>
> *If I had to be a cookie {dog, bird, toothpaste, automobile, fairy tale character, public figure, movie actor/actress, etc.]*
>
> *I remember when*
>
> *When I close my eyes sometimes*
>
> *Have I told you how. . . ?*

What's-istina. I can't think of a name for this reasonably simple form of poetry. It's adapted from the sestina, a comparatively difficult form I won't explain here. I've used what follows with youngsters on many occasions. Most kids like to play with its possibilities and are intrigued with how a little clutch of unrelated words distributed to everyone in common generates markedly different meanings from poet to poet. The what's-istina, like most other forms delineated in this section, lends itself obviously enough to group effort and is as well quite suitable for solitary pursuit. I like the form. It's easy, tends to result in attractive poems, and gives reluctant poets a ready chance to observe their own poetic creativity in action.

It works like this (my version, anyhow; work out your own variations to suit): jot down four-word lists of nouns, verbs, adjectives or adverbs; or mix them up, one of each. don't attempt to *compose* lists; pull words out of the air; copy them randomly from the newspaper, the Yellow Pages, a novel, a piece of junk mail. I'd avoid the absurd, the silly, unless the evening is to be devoted to cooking up absurd, silly poems. Poets are to create two four-line stanzas. In the first stanza each line ends with one of the four words. The same is true of the second stanza, except that the order is reversed: if you ended the first line of stanza one with, say, "aardvark," then "aardvark" must be used to end the *last* line of stanza two. But this all sounds much more confusing than it really is. Here are some examples that should make the idea clear. They were written by youngsters ages twelve to fifteen in approximately twenty minutes. The list of words I gave them: *bell, rain, garden, glass.* They were told that they must use the words in that order.

His ego rang out like a church bell,
It bloomed after a light spring rain,
And was as beautiful as a flower in a well-tended garden.
It was so clear and distinct as to resemble glass.

But many times dusty grows the glass,
And the flower wilts no matter how well-tended the garden.
And where lightning strikes and Mother Nature conjures rain,
The rust overtakes the once-proud bell.

* * *

The fragments of the tiny ornamental bell
Scattered in the downpour of rain
Littering the large English garden
With small splinters of fractured glass.

Down from the window came large shards of glass
Filling the small, apartment garden
Like droplets of pouring rain ·
On the city prized for a large cracked bell.

* * *

Listen to the ringing bell.
A claxon call in the pouring rain,
Its cry resounding through the garden,
Its cry calling at you through the glass.

You can come through the streaked glass,
Answering the call in the garden.
You can skip through the pouring rain,
You can stay and listen to the bell.

* * *

Listen! Can you hear the bell,
Muted, softened by the rain?
Look beyond; the dripping gardens
Through this rain-washed window glass.

Like tear-stained pictures under glass,
Vistas of the shabby gardens
Melt and mingle with the rain
And the tremor of the bells.

Try one. *Now.* Just to see how it works; you don't have to share it with anyone else. Here—*books, kiss, ache, river.* Give it half an hour. (When's the last time you did something as decadent—and worthwhile—as playing at poetry for one forty-eighth part of a day?)

Cottage Poems. Here is a gathering of writings I've saved for last in this section. They're not tidily classifiable. Are they group poetry? journal-keeping of a sort? a form of ongoing dialogue among family members? Yes. The Ful-wiler family (you've met them elsewhere in this book)—Toby, Laura, Megan (then 12), and Anna (8)—use writing to amuse, harmonize, convey affection, idle away a rainy hour, gather up memorable moments before they're forgotten. They're a family of writers—in this instance, writers at their summer cottage on Lake Superior—doing exactly what writers are supposed to do and obviously enjoying it.

Cottage Poems is a homegrown, homemade 12-page booklet. Some of the selections are rounds, poems of the kind discussed on p. 123, where each participant contributes a line or two, then passes the work on to the next poet. Here are examples. (Lines are unattributed.)

Sailboats

White sails hover, waiting for wind
White sails are scary to me
White sails fluttering, scary, hovering, playing
White sails bring wind thoughts
White sails will rise again next summer

Slumber Parties

Seven girl-women float on the beach in cotton nightgowns.
Mom and Dad peek out the window of
the cottage and smile quietly at each other.
Seven smiles, sticky marshmallow lips smile for more.

I hardly got to do any of the things
they did.

You, younger daughter, will soon have beach parties, treasure hunts,
and birthday friends who will whisper to you long after Mom and
Dad are fast asleep.

The following is a variation on the name poem described on page 124. (Note the use of poetic license in line five.)

Stairs squeak and are soft.
Tip-toeing up them when I'm supposed to be in bed
Alarms my parents, excites my dog.
I pad through the hall, stomach grumbling.
R stairs crunch when you walk.
Stairs are fun.

Even when poems were individually composed, titles were provided by other family members. Eight-year-old Anna named this poem by her father "Planting."

All winter long
the lake slept
the flowers died
the cottage was cold.

And all spring long
the lake thawed
the flowers grew
the cottage was warm.

Not all the writing took the cottage or the season for its subject. Megan's "Lipstick" ("Title from Mom") raises a question that seems too large to fit into a summer.

Lipstick is to me the object of the
older world.
I will walk into Roy's
testing perfume and pink eyeshadow,
gazing at the rainbow array
of lipstick — wondering when
I too will belong in the
older world.

And Anna's "Cart-Wheels" has all the breathless exuberance of a cartwheel itself.

Cart - wheels

Cant-wheels are fun to do

~~Cart-wheels~~

I had trodle learing how

when I first leaned I couldn't stoq

I still can't stoq doing them

I Like makeing shows with capt-wheels

The best writing isn't that which wins prestigious awards or reaps fortunes for its author; it is simply that which is to and for those we care most about.

EPITAPHS
A mostly neglected form of short verse is the epitaph. I recommend your recommending epitaph writing to your family, children over ten included (and even younger if they show early signs of drollery). The inducements? Epitaphs average only four lines, making their composition a matter of a few inspired moments. Additionally, they'll bring out the very best of the writer that lives in us, for epitaphs are meant to be chiseled in stone, after all, and that is no medium for second-raters. They also offer writers an opportunity to make unrebuttable observations about their subjects. And who wouldn't rather write his or her own epitaph rather than leave it to some uncaring tombstone chiseler?

This isn't a grim exercise. The most memorable epitaphs throughout history have had a wry twist to them, and some are downright funny, even in cold stone. Here are three, all on the corny side, simply to provide rough models and rhyme schemes. In terms of tone and form they're quite like the limerick, although note that examples one and two have alternate line rhyme, while example three has the same end rhyme throughout. Note also that while the standard first line in epitaphs seems to begin, "Here lies . . . (in the limerick it's "There once was. . ."), the third example doesn't. In other words, feel free to experiment.

Here lies baby Elinor
who never cries nor hollers.
She only lived for 30 days
and cost us 20 dollars.

* * *

Here lies Jason Maces
Who played his poker sharp.
Til once he played 5 aces,
and now he plays a harp.

* * *

Under this stone lies Horace Blue
Who owned a pistol, a thirty-two.
To see if it was dirty, into it he blew.
The gun went off and he did too.

POEMS FROM US TO THEM

Lois Duncan, a highly successful writer of young adult novels, told me recently that she had composed a lullaby for a new grandchild.

"I wrote one too," I said, "for our first child."

"What did you do with it?" she asked.

"Well, I don't know. . . I mean I'm no songwriter. I guess I just sort of made it up in my head and let it go at that."

Lois had done it the right way. She's not a songwriter either. She's a dedicated parent who happens to know the value of written words in a family context. So she wrote down the lyric and asked a friend to put the words to music. The final step was recording the lullaby, which she did to guitar accompaniment.

We're all capable of creating uncomplicated lyrics. Admit it, you've written dozens of songs in your head. Furthermore, nearly everybody knows somebody capable of translating your hummed or plunked-out notion for a tune into notes on a musical staff; and once that's accomplished, it will be easy enough to draft a guitar-playing friend and a trio of family members to vocalize. Who wouldn't be delighted to receive such a gift, whatever the occasion?

I trust that this letter, written by my daughter, then in her junior year at college, won't need any explaining.

Dear Dad,

I spent most of yesterday cleaning out the desk in the living room. The best thing I found was something you never gave me. It's an old, yellowed piece of paper that's dog-eared and coffee stained. I'd send it to you but it's such a sweet little thing that I'm going to try to fix it up and frame it. You must have written it when I was a little girl. Why didn't you ever give it to me? Here it is:

For Laura, my daughter, who is fast aging into loveliness, because you asked me to write you a prayer of your own.

I look up at laughing brothers
In a green-dappled tree
And thank You, when I think of it,
For letting me be me.

Here, another parent recalls sending her daughter off to school. It would be good, I think, to reflect for a moment after reading Susan Casper's "First-Day-of-School Quiet" on what a rich and loving gift she has offered, and how, unlike a toy or a piece of clothing, it will never break or wear out or fall from style.

First-Day-of-School Quiet

But you
come hurrying back
to kiss me goodbye
(almost forgotten
both of us so grown.)
You, half child-half woman
with backpack slung over one shoulder
ankles wobbling
fragrant with perennial first-day smells:
new erasers, #2 lead, and fresh crayons.
Me, half woman-half child,
rising to my toes
so we won't notice
you've reached my height.

I pull wilted chrysanthemums
one-by-one
from a chipped vase
then climb the stairs
to find your bedspread smooth.

CHAPTER SEVEN

Equipping a Place for Writers to Write

While this chapter probably won't excite, it may electrify, for it has mainly to do with things that go blink—writing's machinery, as well as its related paraphernalia and a place to put it all. No hard evidence exists to establish positive, cause-and-effect connections between the hardware and/or ambience for writing and what comes out. If anything, the opposite suggests itself: extremes of deprivation and misery often have figured in the writing of masterpieces. All I can say is that I've tried it both ways, and while neither seems to work, I continue to lean toward comfort and convenience, despite my Yankee upbringing. This brief chapter on equipping a place for writers to write could run you between two and eight thousand dollars to read and guarantees nothing in return other than the probability that by following its suggestions you'll encourage writing in the home.

WORD PROCESSORS

Jim Collins, who teaches at the State University at Buffalo, knows enough about word processors to have edited a book about their uses in education. I've had reason to consult him of late, for my computer is no longer reliable, and I've decided to get a new one. In fact, what moved me to call him is that a couple of weeks back I lost four days' worth of work on this book. An emergency arose out in the barn, and I dashed down there to remedy it. In my absence, a vagrant little runt of a lightning bolt wiped out nearly 16 pages of text. The repairs cost about two hundred dollars. The machine still isn't right.

The computer Jim recommends costs approximately as much as I paid for a brand-new Volvo sedan back in the early sixties. It's priced at about what I'd spend today to purchase fifteen electric typewriters equivalent to the one I'm using now—the one I dragged out of the closet after the lightning struck.

Typewriters don't erase what's on them when the power goes haywire. Neither do they cause eyestrain nor require the use of jargon to discuss. (Typewriters are not much more discussable than hatchets.) They do not attract know-it-alls stuffed to the gills with unsolicited observations such as, "Only a damn fool would go to the barn without punching the save key first."

The other reason I called Jim was to ask for suggestions about what to say on the general subject of word processors and family writing. He sent me an article he had just completed and invited me to quote from it. I'll do that gladly, inasmuch as his position on the subject is much more clear-headed and unbiased than is my own at the moment. (But I'll stick in my two cents' worth too.)

> Helping children learn to write can be enhanced by using home computers as tools for writing. Because the computer facilitates mechanical aspects of the writing process, more time and energy can go into the real work of writing. And because computers make it easy to change what's written, revising and editing are considerably easier than when composing by hand.
>
> Relative freedom from tedium is the real advantage of word processing. This is writing in a new and welcome medium for young children: there's no pencil to grasp, no paper to keep from sliding, no eraser to wear a hole in the paper, no lines to stay on, and best of all, no copying over for neatness. For older kids, too, writing with computers is more inviting than writing by hand. Words can be pushed out of the way by new words, or new words can zap away the old ones. Sentences and paragraphs can grow or shrink, stay put or move, become linked or separated. Changes can be tried and kept, saved and printed, or they can be discarded at any step along the way.

I agree. It *is* easier, less tedious to use a word processor than it is to write in longhand or with a conventional typewriter, even an electric model like this one. And kids do seem to be drawn to computerized writing, in the main for reasons Jim cites just above, but also, I believe, because it's exciting to see your words *materialize* on the screen. (It isn't nearly as much fun to sit there and watch them vanish.) Part of the fascination with word processing, I'm convinced, stems from young people's general fascination with computers— with the joysticks, the blinking lights and *Star Wars* sound effects, the raw speed of their micro-chip mentalities. Loosely, at least, the act of writing with a word processor is, especially for the young, a futuristic one. It has no equivalent; while we can readily perceive the evolutionary connections between a typewriter and the earliest of writing instruments and comprehend the scribal techniques of any age, writing with a computer seems relative to no other medium in history. And for this reason—and perhaps too because the printing and the margins are wonderfully neat so that what the printer prints looks nearly like the pages in a book—it is easy to assume that something in the bowels of this miraculous machine makes the words come out *better* than they would laboriously formed with a pencil. It probably does little harm to believe this.

Because word processing makes it easier to produce and revise writing, it also makes it easier for parents to help children with their writing. We can adopt a "Let's see how this works" attitude, knowing that changes need be only tentative until we see how they look. We can move sentences and paragraphs around to see if organization improves. We can help children correct usage and mechanical problems right on the screen, and we can work on one problem at a time, such as first correcting the capitalization errors, then the comma errors, all the while knowing that no recopying will be needed.

As Jim points out elsewhere in the article, parents and word processing software both can nevertheless go overboard on drills and practice designed to address the correction of mechanical flaws, also and erroneously referred to as "grammatical errors." Whether or not a term is correctly capitalized usually has nothing much to do with its meaning or effectiveness. Furthermore, being "correct" (an impossibility in the first place) shouldn't be confused with writing well, anymore than being able to name a horse's anatomical parts should be mistaken for the ability to ride. Consider too that kids get plenty of drilling in school. Administered heavy-handedly at home, it may drive youngsters away from what parents should most want them to learn to cherish—the pure act of writing. Jim's let's-see-how-this-works approach, administered with a light and loving hand, is the only sensible way to deal with matters of correctness.

It's hard to find a word processor these days that isn't a darned good writing tool. What features should we look for in a word processing program for school-aged children? Three basic features are especially important: simple command structure, logical command structure, and easy file loading and saving. A simple command structure uses only one or two keystrokes [for editing, formatting, and printing]. A logical command structure keeps commands out of the way until needed. . . . Easy file loading and saving is necessary because beginning word processing users are easily confused when saving and retrieving files....

We recommend word processors that allow variations in type sizes and styles. Children like to employ variety for cover pages, titles, and headings. This can be a strong motivation for writing. For the same reason, we recommend underline, boldface, and double width capabilities.

Had I read the uncomplicated advice above just a few years ago, it would have made absolutely no sense to me. When I bought my computer, I had no idea that word processors are *programs;* I thought they were machines. (There are word processing machines, too. They fall somewhere between conventional typewriters and computers. By comparison to the latter, they're extremely limited in function.) I didn't know how to get my computer to write or even what the simple term *file* meant in the context of word processing. No one back then could have convinced me that I could get such a complicated, inscrutable machine to obey me. And although I don't know much more now than I did then, it long ago became clear that one needn't. It doesn't take technical know-how nor long study to use a word processor. Anyone who knows the alphabet and has sufficient manual dexterity to poke a key is, theoretically at least, capable of computer-assisted writing.

What Jim's advice means, for those readers as ignorant about this business now as I was then, is that a word processing program that youngsters can work with comfortably shouldn't be complicated or illogical. (Computers themselves are no more complicated to run than the average flashlight: depending on which way you flip the switch, they are either on or off.) A "command structure" is the way the program's designers have set up instructions that allow you to request certain operations to be performed. If, for example, I want to type with an unjustified (ragged right) margin, I hit two keys, O and X. To return to a justified margin, I hit two others. To center a line, such as a poem title or subheading, requires my hitting the O and C keys. Bang! The line leaps to the center of the screen faster than a frightened hare. To erase a line involves hitting the Y key. There are plenty of other commands too, most of which I don't bother with but at least half of which are simple enough for a young child to learn and apply.

I've always found the term *file* to be misleading, even offputting. The label applies to any separate piece of writing and not, as it once did, to an overstuffed cream-colored folder stored alphabetically in a cabinet of the same name. If Edgar Allan Poe had owned a word processor, he would have had to start a file called "The Raven" before he could have pecked out "Once upon a midnight, dark and dreary, . . ." In other words, you can't simply turn the machine on and begin typing, as you can with a typewriter. If Poe had wanted to continue next day banging away at the same poem, he would have first typed in a simple command. In response, something like "What file do you want?" would appear on the screen. He'd type in "The Raven" again, and whatever he had written the day before under that heading would materialize in a wink, ready for additions, deletions, or revision. Had he felt too weak and weary for more of the same and wished to begin another poem, he might have typed "To Helen," or "The Bells." He would then be greeted by a blank screen awaiting his words.

Saving a file—the equivalent of removing a page from your typewriter and inserting it in one of those cream-colored folders for safekeeping—is vital. Hence Jim's cautionary advice. Had Poe simply shut down his machine after the last "Nevermore," forgetting to issue a *save* instruction, American literature would have been the poorer for his negligence. With my program all it takes is typing a *K* and a *D*. When the computer receives this command, it logs into its memory everything in the file I've been working on. Forget the KD and you're a goner. Obviously enough, the simpler it is to call up (retrieve) and/or save a file, the less chance for confusion, frustration, occasional disasters.

Printers produce on paper what you have stored in a particular file. One keystroke and up pops the query, "Name of file to be printed?" Just under this is a listing of every file housed on the diskette in the machine's maw. "Galoshes," I tell it, and in response it raises some simple questions about how I want the printing of that file to come out. I answer each by tapping the space bar, which in effect tells the machine, "Go ahead and print the bloody thing the standard way; don't pester me with details."

"Zizz-zizz," the printer responds, its print head racing back and forth across the page spewing out letters. (Some printers go clickety-click, while some of the pricey models are eerily quiet.) For most writing requirements there is almost nothing to learn about printers other than whether or not they're compatible with the computer and word processor you plan to use. Like a computer, a printer has an on-off switch, and beyond that a few simple externally adjustable what's-its. Some printers produce what's called "letter quality" type.* Mine doesn't, yet I've sent out at least two thousand letters printed on the thing and nobody has complained about neatness or legibility. (There

---

*So-called laser printers are vastly more versatile, powerful, and expensive than the typical home or small office printer. You don't need one.

are printers, though, that do such crude work you wouldn't want to use one to run off a grocery list. The obvious applies: don't buy one.)

While few homes actually need a word processor, it isn't entirely sensible to dismiss them as a frill. I long resisted persuasions from friends, spouse, and kids to get one—I am in the writing business, after all—but I'm not always sorry that I finally gave in. It does make the physical act of composing easier. Furthermore, if one believes the pundits, learning is gradually becoming more a family function and less a school-centered process; and computers are part of learning's growing body of technological tools. In the large suburban high school at the foot of the mountain, for example, typing classes are taught not with typewriters but with computers. Eventually, I'd guess, any kid who isn't reasonably adroit with a keyboard by age eight is going to suffer a far worse handicap than I did as a lefty at that age.

Here, in stripped-down form, are the chief advantages and drawbacks of ownership as considered from a family writing perspective.

Pluses

As noted, kids love computers, tend to find writing with them less laborious. (Never a need to copy over.) The same applies to adults too. (Whoever invented the notion that only kids make errors, have need to revise?)

Typing with a computer keyboard is virtually noiseless. This is a wonderful advantage over a conventional typewriter, allowing for late-night or early A.M. writing. It also allows for work in the same room with other family members who may be studying, chatting, watching tv, or snoozing.

A relatively new type of machine, the laptop, runs on batteries or a/c, weighs just a few pounds, and has a screen bright enough to be read in nearly any light. Laptops work where handwriting doesn't—under jouncy

Minuses

You can't provide every child in a household with a computer. Even the cheap ones are expensive. There's a good chance that there'll be occasional bickering unless a schedule is worked out in advance and held to. And count on all hell breaking loose when one child damages the machine or erases someone else's work. Best to insist on each kid using only his or her diskettes.

It's downright impossible to select the best hardware and/or software for your family's purposes. There are simply too many makes and models, too many programs—each boasting features and gimmicks enough to make your head spin. Most of the literature is too densely jargonized and technical to make sense of. The average computer salesperson doesn't understand it either.

conditions, such as in a car or plane. Their eminent portability provides additional benefits that are easy enough to figure out. (Despite what salespeople say, the typical small computer isn't truly portable, just luggable.)

To stray from the writing context for a moment, let me point out what nearly everyone already knows: computers can do lots of other things besides drive word processing programs. They can help you balance your checkbook, run a business, help teach you how to fly an airplane, or lay out a floor-plan for an addition on the house. Furthermore, there are countless tutorial programs designed for youngsters and adults, as well as dictionaries, thesauruses, and many more specialized reference sources. And don't forget games, ranging from those appropriate to preschoolers up to extremely demanding ones.

Using a modem, you can hook your machine up to a telephone and receive and send typed copy directly over the wires. This is of value for students, clearly enough, but it has other uses too, from sending off an emergency recipe to participating with off-premises friends and relatives in many of the writing-centered activities described elsewhere in this book. Such computer hook-ups, it has been found, tend to encourage both children and adults to engage in more writing than they otherwise

Not only are computers expensive to buy, they're also expensive to fix. My machine, highly recommended at the time of purchase and used relatively lightly, has run up over $600 in repairs, nearly all the result of five years' normal wear and tear.

Computers decrease in value at an alarming rate. This can be a decided plus if you're shopping for a used one, but not if you've decided to upgrade and wish to sell your present model. (Nor is there a reliable way to determine how much use/abuse a used computer has had.)

Sooner or later and no matter how cautious you are, your computer is going to zap you, just as mine did.

Although some programs are in the public domain—free for the copying, that is—most of the truly good ones are not. Yes, you can find a program today that will allow you to perform nearly any operation you can think of, along with a vast array of resource materials, games, and whatnot. But you can run through a pile of money in the process. Studies of computer use in homes have indicated that interest in and employment of self-help programs wane rather rapidly. (If you hate to balance your checkbook, you'll hate it just as much using a computer.) Ditto, games. What's wrong with playing checkers the old-fashioned way, anyhow?

I don't care what the experts say, staring at a computer screen is bad would. And because a number of writers may participate at the same time, collaborative composing is a common practice. The implications for a family writing network are exciting.

A word processor, especially if it is designed to be used by the very young, can encourage kids to write earlier in life than they might otherwise do, and can also, through various enhancements, help sustain their interest in composing.

Jim's article makes reference to a word processor that talks. The child presses a letter key and the computer speaks the letter without printing it. If it's the desired letter, the child presses the key again and the letter appears on the screen. This isn't meant to amount to an exercise in spelling; its virtue is that it helps youngsters coordinate eye, ear, and touch in a language-making context. It also assists a child in achieving what he or she is passionately keen about: producing writing to be shared.

for your eyes. My vision, always good, was just settling into a gentle, middle-age decline when I bought my machine. I've had three progressively stronger lens prescriptions since and am in need of still another. After a session at the word processor, my vision invariably stays blurred for fifteen minutes or so.

Modems don't necessarily encourage the kind of prose that deserves to be called writing. I've heard numerous complaints from parents that kids tie up the phone for maddeningly long stretches cranking out written prattle or copying each other's homework. And because writing is slower than talking, big phone bills get run up.

Little kids should be encouraged to form their own letters, scribe their own stories, notes, poems; and never, ever should it be suggested to them that what they "write" isn't intelligible. What you're "reading" are the shapes of your child's eager imagination. To learn, to discover, involves at an early age drawing the thoughts and images that swarm in the mind. Furthermore, there is hand and eye coordination to consider. Not to be mistaken with "penmanship," symbol-making is important to a child's self-image and peer group status. It's doubtless neater to use symbols encoded in a program, but it isn't necessarily better.

Much, much more might usefully be said on the subject of word processors but (a) I don't know all that much, and it struck me that since you may not either, my ignorance-based brevity is appropriate; (b) anything more complex/technical that might have been included would date so fast as to be next to useless within a few months of this book's publication (indeed, is quite dated already); and (c) it's a terribly dull subject no matter how one approaches it.

Had home computers been available when my kids were young, I'd doubtless have invested in one. Today, in fact, they aren't all *that* expensive. Since I bought my model, not only have prices dropped, but quality and versatility have increased dramatically, as has the range of programs, many of them no more costly than a video movie. But don't let anyone buffalo you into believing it takes more than paper, a pencil, and some systematic encouragement to get writers of any age to write. And discount or dismiss any hype from salespeople or ads about how micro-chip devices can increase your vocabulary or improve your spelling. The only way to accomplish either is through reading and writing.

COPY MACHINE

That there are probably a thousand videocassette recorders in private homes for every copy machine is one more proof that our priorities are skewed. You can buy an untemperamental, easy-to-use copier for as little as what a state-of-the-art VCR costs. It won't require smelly chemicals, special paper, or frequent servicing, nor will it take up much more space than a breadbox. Sure, you can run down to the copy shop or sneak some stuff through the office copier, but neither is as practical as having a machine on your own premises, especially with a houseful of writers.

My compact, affordable copier won't play movies or record tv shows, but it will make a crisply legible copy every 7 seconds, print up to 20 copies automatically, reproduce photographs (although far from perfectly), and copy both sides, using standard or legal-size paper. Its carriage is designed to accommodate open books and magazines, the machine can be set up to print in various colors, and its operator's manual offers the clearest instructions I've ever read.

Elsewhere throughout this book I've asked readers to use writing as a means of learning, discovering. Here, let it serve as a medium for convincing yourself that your family needs a copier. Along with any family members young or old that you can snare, write nonstop a list of copier applications that pertains to the household. It isn't necessary to stick to family writing concerns; they'll surface on their own. Write for ten minutes, just to see what happens. Don't bother with complete sentences; one- or two-word jots should do for the most part, as in "poems," "legal documents," "clippings," etc.

You'll want to compare lists, of course. And think how easy that would be if you had a copier!

THE WRITER'S CORNER

William Faulkner wrote his first novel in longhand on an upturned trash can in a boiler room. I wrote my first (and last) novel, also in longhand, out in Long Island Sound, bobbing up and down on a small, smelly motorboat. My novel was miles worse than Faulkner's, but his wasn't all that good either. I lay our relative failures to the circumstances. Neither of us had enough sense to seek out a more congenial place to write, a quiet, well-lighted, civilized retreat, a writer's corner. It needn't be an actual corner, or course—just a place demarcated by either real or imagined boundaries where the focus is on writing.

Ideally, you already have the space—a lightly used den, a spare bedroom, an area in the basement or attic that can be partitioned off. While it's physically possible—even perhaps classifiably an American tradition—to compose at the kitchen table, what this suggests is that writing's place in the home is temporary and furthermore that writing is necessarily a casual and inconsequentially public act, to be performed amidst clatter and traffic. American homes have tv rooms, recreation rooms, sewing rooms, workshops, each suitably furnished and accoutered. That relatively few homes provide similarly exclusive spaces for writing amounts to a statement of sorts, the kind our kids hear loudly and clearly. Having a "study" on the premises doesn't count. The term was invented by realtors as a snooty way of labeling a room too small to accommodate anything larger than an occasional thought. If you have such a room, stop calling it by that silly name, paint it in bright colors, and fill it with the following:

Paper, paper, paper: all kinds, including lined and unlined writing paper in various colors, notebook paper, small scratch pads, steno pads, note/memo pads, self-stick notes; construction paper, bristol board, calligraphic paper, greeting card blanks (expensive till you compare what a store-bought card costs); letter stencils and peel-and-stick letters; envelopes, including some 9 x 12 clasp-type.

I also want to argue here in favor of the following: a return address stamp or self-adhering address stickers to be provided for every family member over age six; and, should you and/or others opt for personalized stationery, an avoidance of the smarmy-cute, uselessly small, kitten-bunny-wildflowers-cluttered note-sized stuff that doesn't afford room enough for even a modest insult. Writing reads best on plain, honest sheets of paper, not superimposed on artwork that may argue with the tone or content of the message.

Filing materials: folders, of course, and depending on what kind you elect to use, labels to identify their contents. There are basically two kinds of folders—those that hang suspended on metal hangers and those that don't. I prefer the former. They're easier to dip into, stay neater, last longer. They also require a compatible filing cabinet. If you have the other kind of cabinet, you're stuck with the other kind of file folder. (Three related items deserve mention here: accordion-type portfolios, a Rolodex address file, and if you have a computer, a diskette tray.)

On the subject of cabinets, I suggest your avoiding cheap, lightweight ones. They're junk, most of them, eager to jam closed, fall apart, buckle, catch fingers on unfinished edges. They're especially vulnerable to youngsters' handling. Furthermore, the drawers are shallow. Get a used office-quality cabinet instead. (While stackable, heavy plastic milk case-type boxes are sold as file containers, they're really for storage, not ready access. Ditto the fiberboard models. Conventional file cabinets may look somewhat clunky, but they work best for convenient storage and retrieval.)

To save space in the writer's corner, you might do as I have: get a couple of 2-drawer cabinets and a length of formica-covered kitchen counter cut to fit your available space. Balance the counter on the cabinets. It makes a grand work/drawing table-desk combination. Not bad-looking either.

A parting comment: filing, quite obviously, should rely on a system. Adopt an uncomplicated one and be firm about requiring everyone's adhering to it. For my money, any such system should include a rule about removing a file from the premises, to wit: anybody who yanks a file inserts in its place a marker identifying the borrower.

Writing implements: While far too many people profess to hating to write—that is, to compose—we seem to be a nation in love with making letters, scribing them on paper. What else will explain our fascination with and the remarkable variety of writing tools? There are ballpoints, rollerpoints, felt tips, markers fat enough to letter billboards down to those that produce a line fine enough to pass for that of the steel-pointed pens of my long-ago childhood.

While I don't suggest your purchasing some of each—I counted 36 separate models of pens in an area stationery/office supply store—most people who write agree that there's an imagined connection between a particular writing tool and the felicity of one's writing. I love to write with fountain pens, although being left-handed I make a terrible mess of it, dragging the heel of that hand (and occasionally my shirtcuff) through the still-wet ink. It's that I like the firm, attractive way the letters come out, a satisfaction impossible to duplicate with a ballpoint pen. In my collection of writing instruments are a couple of Rapidograph pens too. They're superb for doing fine lettering and sketching, I find. Allow for family members differing in their taste in pens and pencils (and—first thing—screw a pencil sharpener to the wall). Youngsters like to color their writing. In fact it's often more drawing than lettering, much as it was in early stages of virtually every individual's writing—much as it was in early stages of our collective literacy. (Ontogeny recapitulating philogeny, I think they call it.) So I'd suggest your keeping on hand plenty of colored pens, pencils, crayons, and felt-tip markers. For related reasons, you might also want to include a calligraphic pen set. They're not expensive and it doesn't take much time or artistic talent to master the basics of this gratifying medium.

Consumable items: tacks, push pins, paper clips, staples, transparent tape, masking tape, erasers, paper cement.

Non-consumable items: stapler, tape dispenser, scissors, paper punch, paper cutter. This last item may not appear to be as essential as preceding ones. I've discovered, though, that we use it frequently enough for me to suggest its use to others. I paid thirty-five dollars for a very solid, medium-size model. It can cut through at least 20 sheets of paper at a time, is a mile more accurate than I am with scissors, is ideal for cutting paper of any thickness into greeting cards, memos, index cards, notes, signs, e.g., DO NOT USE PAPER CUTTER WITHOUT PERMISSION, makes a gratifying *screee-unnnk* sound that reminds me of rainy days in second grade, and has even been put to occasional use slicing pepperoni.

I almost forgot clipboards, which of course don't belong in the writer's corner but could be stored there. Clipboards in turn brought to mind a wise observation I read somewhere recently: that instead of throwing out that old briefcase we should give it to a young child. Like the clipboard, it's a symbol of the serious, adult business of writing. (Nearly as portable as a clipboard and twice as easy to write on is the lap desk, a fiberboard tablet that rests on the writer's knees and is lined underneath with beanbag-like cushioning.

Furnishings: Aside from file cabinet(s) and a desk/work table, you'll need some open shelves for books, assortments of paper, and tools of the trade. The adjustable kind fitted to metal tracks screwed to the wall are relatively inexpensive, easy to install, and plenty strong. I also use a type of ready-made bookcase relatively new to the market. These sturdy, inexpensive hardwood units have three shelves nearly a foot deep by thirty inches long, can be stacked two high, and fold flat for storage.

My computer sits at one end of my desk. Had I room for a computer stand, however, I'd buy one in a minute. They're available in cheap but sturdy, assemble-yourself form, house all the computer components and provide some desktop space as well. When I'm not using my machine it sits there, blank-eyed and obtrusive, taking up needed space. With the arrangement I've just described, the computer can be pushed out of the way when not in use.

Especially if writers of different ages will be using the corner, an adjustable chair is a must. Like a clipboard or old briefcase, a genuine office chair will suggest to youngsters that they're truly in the writing business.

My copy machine sits atop one of those pressed-board tv carts on wheels with the fake woodgrain finish. It's just the right height and surface area for the copier, and below are two deep shelves, ideal for storing paper, books, and an oddlot assortment of stuff, including the paper cutter.

I get by with just one of those clip-on, swing-arm desk lamps that looks as if it were made from an Erector set. Because it is designed to tilt and swivel, I'm able to direct its beam and proximity to suit most applications.

I've said nothing here about typewriters for a simple reason: if you don't have a typewriter, it's almost certainly because you don't know how to type. That being the case, I wouldn't get one either. Conversely, if you do have a typewriter, you know as much about them as I do, probably more.

I can't think of anything else to put in your writer's corner except a couple of dogs. I've trained one of mine to pick up whatever drops from the desk and give it to me. The other lies on my feet, which come January is about the best damned trick I can think of for a dog to do.

CHAPTER EIGHT

More Reasons to Write

Inasmuch as previous chapters provide more reasons, invitations, and opportunities to write than you can possibly use up in a lifetime, this little concluding collection of activities isn't necessary or integral to anything that precedes it. Furthermore, this gathering is an arbitrary one: I could just as readily have stuck in a dozen or a hundred alternative activities without adding to or detracting from the chapter's value. These are amusements of the kind you and other family members should be cooking up by now—frivolous diversions, forms of play. For me, this concluding chapter provides a release from all this writing about writing; for you, the chance to write instead of read.

ALPHABET BOOKS

I borrowed the art on page 162 from a graduate student at Michigan State long enough to make a machine copy of a page from the alphabet book he and his three-year-old son were constructing. "Craig does most of the work," his father told me. The "work," I ascertained, involves the boy's hunting up in magazines, posters his parent bring home from work and school, on cereal boxes, wherever, the appropriate capital letter in a shape and color that catch his eye. With help from his mother or father, he cuts the letter out and glues it to a page. "There's an order to it," his father said. "This week it's I think 'J' he's after. If he comes up with a 'W,' we'll lock him in the attic." (Craig doesn't have the alphabet down pat yet, neither its order nor all its letters. But he has a children's chalkboard with the ABC's printed across the top and is able to recognize from these conventional letter shapes the sometimes more stylized versions appearing in other printed sources.)

With the letter pasted in place on a 7"x11" bristol board page, parents and son muse aloud about what illustration should accompany the letter. "He seems to be learning letter sounds," his father said, "although we're not

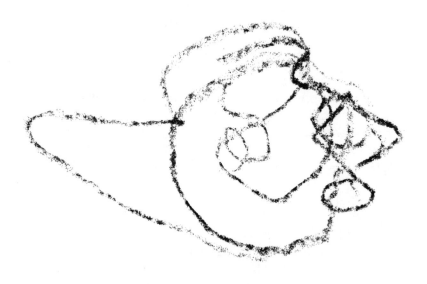

pushing him. If he wanted to draw a car to go with the letter 'T,' we'd probably tell him to draw a Toyota." Mother or father then prints out the name of the illustration.

A simple, useful project admitting of endless variations: a gift produced for a younger sibling by an older one, an alphabet book compiled by grandparents depicting artifacts or pastimes from their own childhood, a scavenger hunt version using only those things that can be found in the child's home.

AUTOGRAPH PARTY

This is possibly the least taxing activity anywhere in the book. It may also be the least purposeful, but it's fun, especially, we've discovered, when a number of people participate. All it requires is a list of well-known people—historical figures, current notables both honorable and notorious, local characters, infamous ancestors, figures from film, fiction, tv, the comics.

Someone, usually whoever cooks up the list, reads off three or four names, allowing perhaps a minute between each. Everyone writes his or her own name exactly as they think the named character would have written theirs. Half the amusement is in translating into a consciously styled signature what we know and feel about the character; the other half comes from comparing styles and arguing about which signature is the most appropriate.

Here are a dozen names to get you started.

Babe Ruth	Minnie Mouse	Wonder Woman
William Shakes- peare	Napoleon	Spiderman
Madonna	Lady Macbeth	Cinderella
Al Capone	Bruce Springsteen	Marilyn Monroe

A slight variation in this activity involves doodling in a hint as to who you are being at the moment. The signatures on page 164 are from four characters on this list.

MONEY MATTERS

In an article on why and how to encourage young writers at home, Mary Adamczyk suggests using writing as a medium for negotiation. What she spells out are sensible ways to deal with pertinent issues in the home as well as providing good grounding for addressing more complicated matters in the future:

Ann Marie McIntyre

Ann Marie McIntyre (or else!)

Marie Ann McIntyre

Ann Marie McIntyre

- Justify an allowance increase with an expense account and budget, perhaps including a savings plan.
- Rationalize a special purchase (say, a hamster or a computer video game).
- Write a complaint letter to a real company, requesting refunds or replacements of defective merchandise.
- Spell out terms for a loan, including a penalty for default (perhaps cooking dinner, depending on culinary skill).
- Negotiate wages for extra chores by submitting a written bid describing the work to be done, benefits, wages, guarantees, and deadlines.
- Submit a resume to parents lucky enough to have more than one child competing for the same task.

BULLETIN BOARD

Most home bulletin/message boards I've seen are put to drably pedestrian uses of the "Harry, set oven at 350" ilk. Nothing wrong with that, I suppose; certainly better than dining on raw chicken. But this only begins to touch on a bulletin board's possibilities, especially in a home filled with writers. Here is a smattering of what else they're good for:

- Quote of the week. Neatly lettered and posted (and removed, to be filed or trashed, at week's end): an off-the-wall observation, e.g., "Wooden stakes are okay, but silver bullets work better. (Old Transylvanian saying)"; an estimable line or paragraph from the news, a book, magazine, or newspaper, whether it's silly, profound, poetic, or simply germane to a family matter of the moment. Not that it has to be current. There's something in *Bartlett's Familiar Quotations* to fit any circumstance. Any home-generated adages, aphorisms, and homilies should be encouraged too, of course, as in, "Don't believe anything wearing a white coat, especially if it offers you ice cream."
- Any short forms of prose or verse, especially home-grown and meant to amuse. This would include limericks, epitaphs, t-shirt slogans, riddles, knock-knock jokes (the last two with answers folded under, as in

    "Knock, knock."
    "Who's there?"
    "Arch."
    "Arch who?"
    — — — — — —
    "Gesundheit.")

- Tom Swifties. But beware. They're catching. After exposure I've caught myself working them into conversations without meaning to. Although TS's are discussed in detail later, here are a couple of examples:

    "Can you lend me a sawbuck?" Tom asked tendentiously.
    "The race is not to the swift," Tom said haltingly.

- Advice column. I've seen this in operation in more than one home. It should probably be played lightly, given the public nature of a bulletin board. Columnists change every couple of weeks. An advice-please envelope is pinned to or nearby the board. Dilemmas, signed with a fictitious name, are deposited for the columnist (also with a fake name) of the moment, who then posts his or her answer in the designated space. I'm not inventing the following exchange between siblings. It cropped up on some friends' bulletin board, and they sent it on to me.

    "Dear Mister Miracles: I'm the shortest person in my class by about 3 inches. What'll I do? (Signed) Under the Weather."

    "Dear Under: Have you thought about staying back?"

- Sniglets. Nearly everyone has cooked up some of these wry/silly words-to-fill-important-gaps-in-the-language, or at very least has chuckled over published collections of them by writer-comic Rich Hall. For those few to whom the term and pastime are new, however, here are a couple of examples:

> *Harshologist:* (noun) A doctor who specializes in telling patients they have two weeks to live.
> *Eyenadequate:* (adjective) Being unable to thread a needle within five tries.

- Nonsensical lists. One week some school kids and I cooked up a list of Indian names. Only two stick in mind, the first because it was part of a newspaper heading: Man Waving Handgun; the second because it's a perfect name for the archetypal medicine man: Old This-Is-Going-To-Sting-a-Bit.

    Carnival and vaudeville acts also beg to be invented and posted, e.g., Captain Dan and His Talking Moustache; Ripcord Rex, the Parachuting Pomeranian; Chester and His Sitting Ducks, etc.

    Ditto rock groups, such as The Ogretones, Comatose, The Laxatives, etc.
- Picture puns don't require any artistic talent whatever, for punsters can find topically appropriate pictures aplenty in magazines to fit their gags. (The two on page 167 are homemade, however.)
- Current letters and cards from far-flung relations and family friends. I also especially like an idea an author friend provided: the posting of machine copied pages from ancestral letters, diaries, journals.
- Writing starters, the notion being that each of you, youngsters and adults alike, will by week's end have produced poem(s), cartoon(s), story, script, somehow reflective of but not necessarily employing verbatim what's posted. I shouldn't be providing such prompts, you should. Here, though, is a mix suggestive of what you might subsequently do.

    Write a letter to the food you hate most.

    A conversation between a stethoscope and a heart.

    "Jack and the Beanstalk" from the Giant's (or goose's) point of view.

    You've stepped inside a cartoon strip and must stay there for a week

There's no sense in going around
with a chimp on your shoulder.

OLD CHINESE SAYING:
WASTE NOT WONTON

(or you've become the newest character on a favorite soap opera or sitcom).

It was his last sight on earth.

I know the speech of whales, and this is what they've told me.

THE NAME GAME

At least three to four notches up the scale from pure silliness, this activity involves any number of participants, each of whom invents a name for a profession/occupation/hobby. The names are to be utterly preposterous, e.g., *Upsidarian, Leaventhropist, Gristickthidian, Olamdumprologist*, etc. Names are either drawn or distributed, and each participant then writes a complete description of his or her moniker, including, for example, information on the history of the profession, its most famous practitioners, how a person becomes one, and why anyone in his/her right mind would want to. Also included is a phonetic spelling out of the term. Participants should additionally be expected to answer the many questions that the curious will raise about being whatever it is you are at the moment. (If you think this doesn't have any language learning significance, think again.)

IN RECOGNITION OF

(So help me, I actually did this.) It's always a safe, sensible bet to honor those citizens who have performed some entirely approvable deed, whether it's heroic, artistic, or philanthropic. But what about those who provide the rest of us with surprise, laughter, even envy for some oddball act, then return to obscurity without so much as a crummy little medal to show for it? It's time somebody did something to honor those unconventional souls we read about in those Associated Press filler items. This idea came to mind many years ago, when my eye fell on an eight-line story about a fellow down in Texas somewhere who had been arrested in a laundromat for stripping naked and stuffing all his clothes in the washer. I thought he deserved some kind of recognition beyond what he got from the judge, so I cooked up an "Above and Beyond Award" and mailed it to Willie Smith in care of the local jailhouse. It never came back, so I figure he must have received it.

No reason why the Jones family shouldn't launch a similar series of awards. (I quit after three, but not because the project soured for me.) Among other things, it will bring out the calligraphic talent in someone in your family, perhaps leading to a lifetime hobby. It will also involve the entire family in reading more thoroughly the human side of the news, and if you take your humor seriously, it will lead to a formally reasoned debate once or twice a month to settle on a recipient. As to what message the award should bear, that, of course, is up to you. I'd suggest making it hifalutin, however — appropriately grandiloquent. Something like this, perhaps: "It is in due recognition of your singular accomplishment [or achievement], to wit, having managed to land your airplane not only at the wrong airport but also in the wrong state, that we the undersigned do hereby proclaim you the Jones Family Citizen of the Month." Etc. Be sure to include lots of scrollwork (which is available in stick-on form at art supply shops) and a gold seal (which I made from a margarine wrapper).

TOM SWIFTIES

As you probably know, Tom Swift was the young hero of a series of novels authored by Victor Appleton back when Wilbur and Orville still owned a bicycle shop. Tom's problem was that he couldn't simply say something, as in, " 'There's a wasp on your nose,' Tom said." His every utterance was modified by an adverb. Thus, it might read something like, " 'There's a wasp on your nose,' Tom said stingingly." Not really, of course. But the obvious pun above *is* based on Appleton's excesses with adverbs, to the point where cooking up lists of so-called Tom Swifties — puns of a type that owe their origin to one writer's stylistic quirk — has become a popular pastime. TS's are fun, and you don't have to have read Appleton to crank out world-class facsimiles of the original goods. (I doubt that more than 2% of Tom Swifties addicts have read as much as a page of him.)

Tom Swifties sessions are becoming a fireside-and-popcorn tradition and thus entirely appropriate to a book with the intent of engendering fireside-and-popcorn writing. All one needs is a handful of adverbs and an ear for punning. Here are a few samples, ostensibly to provide you with some models but actually because I enjoy cooking them up:

"I just stubbed my toe," Tom said limply.
"May I borrow your stethoscope?" Tom asked heartily.
"I've been on a diet," Tom said thinly.
"Where did you hang the calendar?" Tom asked weakly.
"Someone's cracked the Liberty Bell!" Tom shouted ringingly.

To introduce the TS pastime to family members, you may want to hand out some starter sentences with a separate list of adverbs to select from, as in

"What happened to the dessert?" Tom asked. . . .
"I'd be glad to train your dog," Tom said. . . .
"Do pass the parmesan," Tom said. . . .
(gratingly, tartly, fetchingly)

DOODLING

Below are random pen tracks across paper. They have no meaning; they are utterly without purpose. But, as I've observed elsewhere, it is apparently impossible for the human mind to live with randomness, to subsist in chaos. Doodling is one way out of it; writing is another, related, way. The following is an exercise in creativity. It is meant to foster the practice of thinking on paper, and therefore it should be done again and again over time until it becomes a natural part of a creative repertoire centering on writing. It's also fun, especially as a group undertaking.

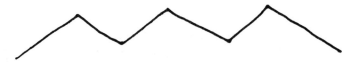

It isn't necessary to make copies of my scribbles; doodle some of your own, keeping them as simple as these. One doodle to a sheet, and leave plenty of room. Pass one out to each family member. The object is to add lines, details until a recognizable subject appears, however crudely. At this point, writing enters into the activity. Each doodler is to name his or her picture and explain in writing the unseen circumstances. How detailed a description is up to the individual. This, for example, is a fleshed-out version of the scribble above, with an accompanying scenario. There are a thousand other possibilities.

This is a clam's eye view of a sunbather asleep on a beach. He wasn't supposed to fall asleep; he was supposed to watch his three little children while his wife went off to buy ice cream cones. When she comes back, she will discover the children far from their sleeping father and will dump his pistachio walnut cone smack on his naked stomach as a way of drawing his attention to his negligence.

Young children especially should be urged to produce doodles for others to respond to. Even pre-schoolers can and should contribute. A parent or older brother or sister can also transcribe for a youngster the story he or she has found in a doodle. It's extremely encouraging for small children to see words and stories of their making appear on paper.

(As an off-shoot of this activity, I fell into creating goofy captioned pictures—the only kind I'm capable of—for my kids to color and add their own details to. One such series involved a collection of unlikely birds, e.g., the blunted bunting [on page 172], the iron-breasted vireo, and the doubtful starter.)

DAYS OF OUR LIVES

Most wall calendars note holidays and commemorative dates. We'd never remember them otherwise, which suggests that most of them are pretty prosaic, or at least that they don't relate importantly to us, just the other guy. There's a way to remedy this, and it's about time we did. Beginning next week (but why not today?) give everyone in your family a week of his or her own, or alternatively a day of each week for a month or so. Each square of the calendar belonging to that person is to be neatly labeled with the owner-contributor's version of a commemorative day and, when practicable, is to be suitably honored by all family members. (It is perfectly reasonable to honor Charlie's Be Kind to Little Brothers Day or Suzie's Night of the Oreo Cookie, while it may not be workable to go along with somebody's Steal a Hubcap Tuesday.) I've seen squares filled with such whimsies as National Electric Eel Day, Waffle Wednesday, Birthdate of Count Dracula, Kiss Somebody with Bad Breath Day, Say No to Everything Day, and Anniversary of the First National Nose-Blowing Championship. This activity can be played straight on occasion too. Nothing wrong with Nobody Grump at Breakfast Day, for example. The point is to fill in at least a month's worth of special days and see what happens.

An offshoot of the calendar idea is the horoscope, where the owner of a week or day posts his or her astrological predictions for family members. Played tongue-in-cheek, it's a perfect opportunity for spoofing. (Played seriously, you risk revealing your lowbrow tendencies.) Here is a list of signs, symbols, and corresponding dates:

Aries (March 21-April 19), the ram
Taurus (April 20-May 20), the bull
Gemini (May 21-June 20), the twins

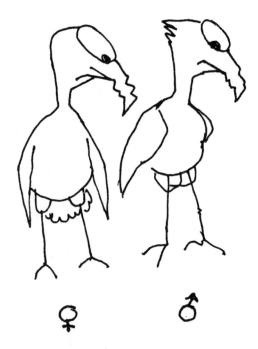

♀   ♂

BLUNTED BUNTING (Fringillidae Ridiculum) 10"
Approximately the size of the red-bellied
woodpecker or the stunted swan. Habitat:
summers, Arctic tundra; winters, shopping malls.
Color: similar to glossy ibis, downcast flycatcher,
but with blotchy underparts. Cry: a drawn-out,
metallic-sounding boiing, somewhat like the
sound that accompanies a telephone operator's
coming on the line. Nesting sites: abandoned
cars, elaborate hair-do's, elevator shafts. Flight
characteristics: flies at objects, rather than
around them, often at high speed. (Blunted
bunting young have beaks approx. 6" long. By the
end of the first year they are approx. 2" long.)

Cancer (June 21-July 22), the crab
Leo (July 23-August 22), the lion
Virgo (August 23-September 22), the virgin
Libra (September 23-October 22), the balance
Scorpio (October 23-November 21), the scorpion
Sagittarius (November 22-December 21), the archer
Capricorn (December 22-January 19), the goat
Aquarius (January 20-February 18), the water bearer
Pisces (February 19-March 20), the fishes

Why not something like this for your Capricorn husband: "A good day to shop for bargains in pearls" or, "Keep those closest to you happy today. Work late," or, "Do what you can to remedy domestic tension. Take your spouse out to dinner"?

Another variant of the calendar project is the greeting card that celebrates an invented day. I've used them too in place of birthday greetings. Two examples are on pages 174 and 175.

INVISIBLE INK

When we were kids we were always passing around notes written in invisible "ink." If I remember correctly it was lemon juice, which was supposed to become readable when you held match or candle under it. It usually didn't work, though, because the paper would catch fire before the message came out. Only recently have I discovered that all it takes is holding the paper over a lightbulb long enough to heat it. Furthermore, any citrus will do, as will milk or sugar water. A small watercolor brush works best as a writing implement.

There are other versions of invisible writing too: you can use pin-pricked letters, which also show up when held to the light. And a friend who specializes in writing instruction recommends that temporary writer's block can sometimes be cured by using two pieces of paper, a sheet of carbon paper, and a wooden stylus. Insert the carbon between the pages and write invisibly on the top one with the stylus. He swears it works. (An alternate version of this practice is to turn off the screen on your word processor and type away in the dark.)

For every use you can come up with for invisible ink (e.g., making resolutions you'd rather not keep), your kids will come up with a dozen.

Happy National Cream of Wheat Day!

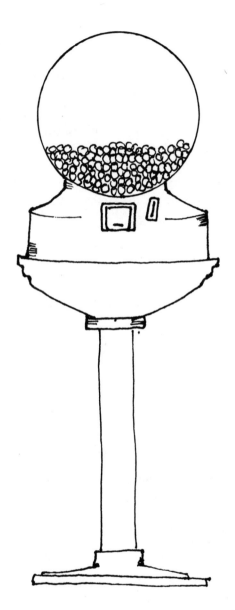

Greetings to somebody lucky enough
to be born on National Gumball Day!!

QUESTIONNAIRES

My seldom-noted survey of practically everyone reveals that as a society we find questionnaires irresistibly engrossing. Indeed, I have unearthed evidence that they were invented by the medical profession to offset the effects of waiting, which was also invented by the medical profession. Why else would doctors' waiting rooms feature so many magazines filled with questionnaires?

Because we are such suckers for them, it should fall to someone in the family—I'd suggest taking turns on a weekly or biweekly basis—to cook up and post on the bulletin board a spoof questionnaire designed to reveal some quality of character, personal tendency, hidden aptitude or aversion. Everybody knows the form, which is a series of short questions preceded by a brief statement of purpose and followed by instructions for determining the results. The wackier the questions, the better. Here's an example from my files:

Is Running for You?

This questionnaire is based on a years-long study of those who jog or run for recreational and fitness purposes. It does not concern itself with those who jog or run for other reasons, such as to flee from the scene of a crime or because they imagine they are being pursued by creatures no one else can see.

YES   NO

_____ _____   1. Have you ever thrown a rock at a bird?

_____ _____   2. When you color, do you try to stay inside the lines?

_____ _____   3. Do you copy down the toll-free numbers in tv ads?

_____ _____   4. Has a zither ever figured importantly in your life?

_____ _____   5. Do you hang things from the rear view mirror?

_____ _____   6. What kind of bird was it?

_____ _____   7. Have you ever bowled over 200 or been in a plane crash?

_____ _____   8. Do you have a favorite nostril? Italian food?

_____ _____   9. Do you believe that you will survive a nuclear attack but nobody else will?

_____ _____   10. Do you have mixed feelings about being unable to make up your mind?

If you answered YES to any two of the questions above, think twice about running. It may not be your cup of tea. (Are you capable of thinking twice? Do you ever fly into a frenzy when a tea leaf sticks to your teeth?) If YES to three or more questions, even a brisk walk with the dog (Do you ever forget your dog's name or whether or not you own one?) could be ill-advised.

Questionnaires can be used to all sorts of good ends. As the text of a greeting card, for example: 1. Have you ever roasted a chestnut by an open fire? 2. Was Jack Frost nipping at your nose? 3. Were the police notified? Etc. As a medium for lighthearted admonishing: 1. Do you have an irrational fear of lawnmowers? 2. If yes, does this fear increase in early summer? 3. Diminish in fall? 4. If yes, is it replaced by an equally irrational fear of rakes? Etc. As an attention-getting way to leave instructions in your absence: 1. Have you ever put out a cat? (10 points for yes, 0 for no.) 2. Does bed-making rank high among your accomplishments? (20 points for yes, 10 points for so-so, 0 for no.)

LAST ITEMS

Neither of us will profit from my going on at length about other possible involvements with writing. Still, as I observed about Mrs. Glover's piece in chapter 5, concluding is a difficult business. I'd like to do so by listing in very short form a few more notions that may strike you as being worthwhile for somebody in your family to tackle. I'll not provide much in the way of detail; furthermore, I'll respond to the urge to be elliptical, as, for instance, in noting that you can make a gift of writing to your house's future occupants, an idea brought to mind by our discovery of a packet of letters dated about a hundred years before we bought the house in whose wall the letters had been hidden.

Do you live near water? It needn't be an ocean; a large pond will do. Anybody would love to find your message in a bottle, even if it doesn't reveal where treasure is buried.

A nightbook: Dreams fade with first light, as do ideas that come in the dark, lines for a poem, epiphanies, resolutions, solutions, recollections. Is there a nightbook on your bedstand, with a pen located where you can find it in the dark?

Auto rallyes and orienteering (a pedestrian version of rallyeing) require a fastidious working-out of written instructions and directions. Read enough about these sports to set up such an event. We've done an auto rallye. It was quite a challenge but well worth the effort.

A writer's grab bag. A box, bag, jar, whatever, into which family members stick strips of paper bearing messages. The one rule is simple enough: anyone removing a message must insert a new one, not put back the one just drawn. What kinds of message are appropriate? Up to you. A quote you've come across that impresses you, a joke, a brief poem—something that will amuse or in some way make pleasant a moment in the recipient's day.

Kids and adults both could/should script and shoot simple stories with either conventional cameras or camcorders. You don't, though, really need a camera. My kids and I spent a highly enjoyable couple of hours one night interpreting some silly dialogues I'd dashed off months back. No props, just a bunch of us sitting there reading aloud. The kind of evening that sticks with parents and children both, and that was occasioned by nothing more than some very ordinary writing.

When gift giving, make at least one present especially appropriate for a writer—pens, stationery, desk lamp, etc.

Once a year pass out literary awards. Not for high grades in English or any other school-related achievements, but for the kinds of writing I've been going on about long enough. Although such awards could be proffered as a gag, I'd suggest your taking this suggestion to heart and being somewhat serious about conveying your esteem. In fact, I think this is a fit request to close with—that you honor your family's writers and their writing.

APPENDIX: GENEALOGY

As I noted elsewhere, we have an expert genealogist in the family. Cousin Rosemary has traveled well past the bare bones, Old Testament, who-begot-whom business and into the inviting byways revealed by her own research. Her findings make for fascinating reading.

I think, though, that you have to work your way through the basics first, and that even the simplest kind of genealogical research is best accomplished with guidance from knowledgeable people and agencies. Rosemary is an accomplished researcher, comfortable with the specialized brand of scholarship she pursues. Most of us are not. My few attempts to follow genealogical charts resulted in bizarre outcomes: sisters married to brothers, uncles to nieces, people having children after they had died—a mishmash of bigamy, incest, and Transylvanian hocus-pocus. I hadn't read a word about genealogy, just plunged in.

I'd advise your taking a more intelligent course of action. For that reason, I've included the following *very basic* information, some of which is borrowed from an attractive, poster-size handout issued by the U.S. Postal Service and titled *Plant a Family Tree.* It recommends beginning with the drawing up of a simple genealogical chart. (A model is provided on pages 182-183.) Take it back as far as possible, using family members, particularly older ones, to help you fill the blanks. Also study family documents—bibles, birth and marriage certificates, military papers, business records, clippings, incidental family papers. This amounts to detective work of a sort, and you'll probably find it enjoyable. Young people should be included in the research and documenting. It will develop a stronger sense of family, and beyond that, knowing something of research techniques is a decided plus for any youngster.

Having filled in the chart as far back as these resources have allowed, you may wish to seek help from these agencies:

The National Archives maintains census, military, naturalization and immigration records, as well as related federal data. The address: The National Archives, Reference Service Branch, Washington, DC 20408-0001.

The National Genealogical Society offers a pamphlet, "Suggestions for Beginners in Genealogy." The Society will send you a copy if you provide a stamped, self-addressed envelope. According to the Postal Service handout, "the society also has many other books and pamphlets. . . on genealogy. A good beginning book [is] *Instructions for Beginners in Genealogy.*" The address: The National Genealogical Society, Educational Division, 4527 Seventeenth St. North, Arlington, VA 22207-2399.

The Church of Jesus Christ of the Latter-day Saints has accumulated the largest collection of genealogical information in the world. For information write to Mormon Family History Library, Genealogical Department, Department P, 35 N. West Temple Street, Salt Lake City, UT 84150-0001.

Other sources of information are the library and city, county, and state genealogical societies. The same is true of historical societies. If you own a computer, you should also investigate available programs dealing with genealogy.

Family

Spouse

NAME _____

BORN WHERE: _____ WHEN: _____

DIED WHERE: _____ WHEN: _____

Your Children

NAME _____

BORN WHERE: _____ WHEN: _____

NAME _____

BORN WHERE: _____ WHEN: _____

NAME _____

BORN WHERE: _____ WHEN: _____

NAME _____

BORN WHERE: _____ WHEN: _____

Father's Brothers and Sisters

NAME _____

MARRIED TO: _____

CHILDREN: _____

NAME _____

MARRIED TO: _____

CHILDREN: _____

NAME _____

MARRIED TO: _____

CHILDREN: _____

NAME _____

MARRIED TO: _____

CHILDREN

YOUR NAME _____

FATHER
BORN:
WHERE:
DIED:
WHERE:

GRANDFATHER
BORN:
WHERE:
DIED:
WHERE:

GRANDMOTHER
BORN:
WHERE:
DIED:
WHERE:

GREAT GRANDFATHER
BORN:
WHERE:
DIED:
WHERE

GREAT GRANDMOTHER
BORN:
WHERE:
DIED:
WHERE:

GREAT GRANDFATHER
BORN:
WHERE:
DIED:
WHERE

GREAT GRANDMOTHER
BORN:
WHERE
DIED:
WHERE

Tree

NAME _____

BORN WHERE: _____ WHEN: _____

NAME _____

BORN WHERE: _____ WHEN: _____

NAME _____

BORN WHERE: _____ WHEN: _____

NAME _____

BORN WHERE: _____ WHEN: _____

Mother's Brothers and Sisters

NAME _____

MARRIED TO: _____

CHILDREN: _____

NAME _____

MARRIED TO: _____

CHILDREN: _____

NAME _____

MARRIED TO: _____

CHILDREN: _____

NAME _____

MARRIED TO: _____

CHILDREN: _____

MOTHER
BORN:
WHERE:
DIED:
WHERE:

GRANDFATHER
BORN:
WHERE:
DIED:
WHERE:

GRANDMOTHER
BORN:
WHERE:
DIED:
WHERE:

GREAT GRANDFATHER
BORN:
WHERE:
DIED:
WHERE:

GREAT GRANDMOTHER
BORN:
WHERE:
DIED:
WHERE:

GREAT GRANDFATHER
BORN:
WHERE:
DIED:
WHERE:

GREAT GRANDMOTHER
BORN:
WHERE:
DIED:
WHERE:

INDEX

Other Books of Interest

Annual Market Books
    Artist's Market, edited by Lauri Miller $21.95
    Children's Writer's & Illustrator's Market, edited by Lisa Carpenter (paper) $17.95
    Guide to Literary Agents & Art/Photo Reps, edited by Robin Gee $15.95
    Humor & Cartoon Markets, edited by Bob Staake (paper) $16.95
    Novel & Short Story Writer's Market, edited by Robin Gee (paper) $19.95
    Photographer's Market, edited by Sam Marshall $21.95
    Poet's Market, by Judson Jerome $19.95
    Songwriter's Market, edited by Brian Rushing $19.95
    Writer's Market, edited by Mark Kissling $25.95

General Writing Books
    Annable's Treasury of Literary Teasers, by H.D. Annable (paper) $1.00
    Beginning Writer's Answer Book, edited by Kirk Polking (paper) $13.95
    Discovering the Writer Within, by Bruce Ballenger & Barry Lane $17.95
    Freeing Your Creativity, by Marshall Cook $17.95
    Getting the Words Right: How to Rewrite, Edit and Revise, by Theodore A. Rees Cheney (paper) $12.95
    How to Write a Book Proposal, by Michael Larsen (paper) $10.95
    Just Open a Vein, edited by William Brohaugh $15.95
    Knowing Where to Look: The Ultimate Guide to Research, by Lois Horowitz (paper) $16.95
    Make Your Words Work, by Gary Provost $17.95
    Pinckert's Practical Grammar, by Robert C. Pinckert (paper) $11.95
    12 Keys to Writing Books That Sell, by Kathleen Krull (paper) $12.95
    The 28 Biggest Writing Blunders, by William Noble $12.95
    The 29 Most Common Writing Mistakes & How to Avoid Them, by Judy Delton (paper) $9.95
    The Wordwatcher's Guide to Good Writing & Grammar, by Morton S. Freeman (paper) $15.95
    Word Processing Secrets for Writers, by Michael A. Banks & Ansen Dibell (paper) $14.95
    The Writer's Book of Checklists, by Scott Edelstein $16.95
    The Writer's Digest Guide to Manuscript Formats, by Buchman & Groves $18.95
    The Writer's Essential Desk Reference, edited by Glenda Neff $19.95

Nonfiction Writing
    The Complete Guide to Writing Biographies, by Ted Schwarz $6.99
    Creative Conversations: The Writer's Guide to Conducting Interviews, by Michael Schumacher $16.95
    How to Do Leaflets, Newsletters, & Newspapers, by Nancy Brigham (paper) $14.95
    How to Sell Every Magazine Article You Write, by Lisa Collier Cool (paper) $11.95
    How to Write Irresistible Query Letters, by Lisa Collier Cool (paper) $10.95
    The Writer's Digest Handbook of Magazine Article Writing, edited by Jean M. Fredette (paper) $11.95

Fiction Writing
    The Art & Craft of Novel Writing, by Oakley Hall $17.95
    Best Stories from New Writers, edited by Linda Sanders $5.99
    Characters & Viewpoint, by Orson Scott Card $13.95
    The Complete Guide to Writing Fiction, by Barnaby Conrad $17.95
    Cosmic Critiques: How & Why 10 Science Fiction Stories Work, edited by Asimov & Greenberg (paper) $12.95
    Creating Characters: How to Build Story People, by Dwight V. Swain $16.95
    Creating Short Fiction, by Damon Knight (paper) $10.95
    Dialogue, by Lewis Turco $13.95
    The Fiction Writer's Silent Partner, by Martin Roth $19.95
    Handbook of Short Story Writing: Vol. I, by Dickson and Smythe (paper) $10.95
    Handbook of Short Story Writing: Vol. II, edited by Jean Fredette (paper) $12.95
    How to Write & Sell Your First Novel, by Collier & Leighton (paper) $12.95
    Manuscript Submission, by Scott Edelstein $13.95
    Mastering Fiction Writing, by Kit Reed $18.95
    Plot, by Ansen Dibell $13.95
    Spider Spin Me a Web: Lawrence Block on Writing Fiction, by Lawrence Block $16.95
    Theme & Strategy, by Ronald B. Tobias $13.95

The 38 Most Common Writing Mistakes, by Jack M. Bickham $12.95
Writer's Digest Handbook of Novel Writing, $18.95
Writing the Novel: From Plot to Print, by Lawrence Block (paper) $11.95

Special Interest Writing Books

Armed & Dangerous: A Writer's Guide to Weapons, by Michael Newton (paper) $14.95
The Children's Picture Book: How to Write It, How to Sell It, by Ellen E.M. Roberts (paper) $19.95
Comedy Writing Secrets, by Mel Helitzer (paper) $15.95
The Complete Book of Feature Writing, by Leonard Witt $18.95
Creating Poetry, by John Drury $18.95
Deadly Doses: A Writer's Guide to Poisons, by Serita Deborah Stevens with Anne Klarner (paper) $16.95
Editing Your Newsletter, by Mark Beach (paper) $18.50
Families Writing, by Peter Stillman (paper) $12.95
A Guide to Travel Writing & Photography, by Ann & Carl Purcell (paper) $22.95
Hillary Waugh's Guide to Mysteries & Mystery Writing, by Hillary Waugh $19.95
How to Pitch & Sell Your TV Script, by David Silver $17.95
How to Write Action/Adventure Novels, by Michael Newton $4.99
How to Write & Sell Greeting Cards, Bumper Stickers, T-Shirts and Other Fun Stuff, by Molly Wigand (paper) 15.95
How to Write & Sell True Crime, by Gary Provost $17.95
How to Write Horror Fiction, by William F. Nolan $15.95
How to Write Mysteries, by Shannon OCork $13.95
How to Write Romances, by Phyllis Taylor Pianka $15.95
How to Write Science Fiction & Fantasy, by Orson Scott Card $13.95
How to Write Tales of Horror, Fantasy & Science Fiction, edited by J.N. Williamson (paper) $12.95
How to Write the Story of Your Life, by Frank P. Thomas (paper) $11.95
How to Write Western Novels, by Matt Braun $1.00
The Magazine Article: How To Think It, Plan It, Write It, by Peter Jacobi $17.95
Mystery Writer's Handbook, by The Mystery Writers of America (paper) $11.95
The Poet's Handbook, by Judson Jerome (paper) $11.95
Powerful Business Writing, by Tom McKeown $12.95
Successful Scriptwriting, by Jurgen Wolff & Kerry Cox (paper) $14.95
The Writer's Complete Crime Reference Book, by Martin Roth $19.95
The Writer's Guide to Conquering the Magazine Market, by Connie Emerson $17.95
Writing for Children & Teenagers, 3rd Edition, by Lee Wyndham & Arnold Madison (paper) $12.95
Writing Mysteries: A Handbook by the Mystery Writers of America, Edited by Sue Grafton, $18.95
Writing the Modern Mystery, by Barbara Norville (paper) $12.95

The Writing Business

A Beginner's Guide to Getting Published, edited by Kirk Polking (paper) $11.95
Business & Legal Forms for Authors & Self-Publishers, by Tad Crawford (paper) $4.99
The Complete Guide to Self-Publishing, by Tom & Marilyn Ross (paper) $16.95
How to Write with a Collaborator, by Hal Bennett with Michael Larsen $1.00
How You Can Make $25,000 a Year Writing, by Nancy Edmonds Hanson (paper) $14.95
This Business of Writing, by Gregg Levoy $19.95
Writer's Guide to Self-Promotion & Publicity, by Elane Feldman $16.95
A Writer's Guide to Contract Negotiations, by Richard Balkin (paper) $4.25
Writing A to Z, edited by Kirk Polking $22.95

To order directly from the publisher, include $3.00 postage and handling for 1 book and $1.00 for each additional book. Allow 30 days for delivery.

Writer's Digest Books
1507 Dana Avenue, Cincinnati, Ohio 45207
Credit card orders call TOLL-FREE
1-800-289-0963
Prices subject to change without notice.

Write to this same address for information on *Writer's Digest* magazine, *Story* magazine, Writer's Digest Book Club, Writer's Digest School, and Writer's Digest Criticism Service.